# THE SAVOYARDS ON RECORD

# THE SAVOYARDS
# ON RECORD

The story of the singers
who worked with Gilbert and Sullivan
and the records they made

## John Wolfson

*A Headlion Book*
PACKARD PUBLISHING LIMITED
CHICHESTER

Copyright ©1985 John Wolfson

A Headlion book, first published in 1985 by
Packard Publishing Limited, 16 Lynch Down, Funtington,
Chichester, West Sussex PO18 9LR.

ISBN 0 906527 25 2 (hard back)
     0 906527 26 0 (paperback)

Phototypeset in Goudy by
Monitor Business Magazine, Hayling Island
Design and layout by Maurice Rapson
Printed and bound in the United Kingdom by
Downland Reprographics Limited, Chichester

# CONTENTS

vi

# ILLUSTRATIONS

All photographs of records are by Marbeth.

# FOREWORD

More than a hundred years passed between the formation of the D'Oyly Carte Opera Company and its dissolution. During this time the performing traditions of the Gilbert and Sullivan operas were supposed to have been sacrosanct, with little change being intentionally introduced into their presentation. Nevertheless, during the course of a century, changes in taste, style, personnel, training and attitude will invariably result in differences of interpretation. One has only to listen to records made at the turn of the century by artists like Scott Russell and Robert Evett to realize that performing styles have changed. Although the gramophone was in its infancy in 1900, enough records were eventually made by singers who had worked personally with Gilbert and Sullivan to give us some idea of how the Savoy Operas were presented by their creators. *The Savoyards on Record* is a survey of these singers and the records they made.

The theatre in London at the turn of the century comprised a much smaller circle of artists than it does today, and perhaps a more volatile one. Performers frequently pursued careers in more than one area. Singers who appeared together at the Savoy in the 1890s often found themselves together ten years later in West End musicals. Opera singers from time to time turned to oratorio, as stars of light opera turned to the legitimate stage and Variety. Old names kept reappearing in new contexts. Of the original Savoyards, only Rosina Brandram remained with the D'Oyly Carte Company from the earliest days to the disbanding of the London company. And even she pursued a career in musical comedy (with many of her former co-stars) after 1903. *The Savoyards on Record* follows the careers of the Savoyards after they left Gilbert and Sullivan, and details the records that they made in their new careers as well.

For years, however, the earliest of these recordings were either ignored, or held in low esteem by collectors, due to the fact that it long had been the custom to play them at incorrect speeds or with needles that reproduced their sounds poorly. It is only recently, with the development of special needles for early gramophone records and the careful determination of the speeds at which they were recorded, that the playback of these discs has become accurate and acceptable to modern ears. Great interest has since developed in the voices of the first generation of Savoyards.

The purpose of this discography has, therefore, been to list all of the known recordings of every artist who performed under the personal direction of Gilbert *or* Sullivan, and who subsequently made records. *The Savoyards on Record* begins with the recordings of Rutland Barrington and

Richard Temple, who appeared in the 1877 production of *The Sorcerer* at the Opera Comique, and comes to a close with the film of *The Mikado*, released in 1939, the last season in which the D'Oyly Carte Company performed under the direction of J.M. Gordon, one of the last stage managers to work with Gilbert.

The discography presents the singers who performed in the Gilbert and Sullivan operas at the Savoy in the order of their first appearance with the D'Oyly Carte Opera Company (or the Comedy Opera Company). Next are listed the singers who appeared in either Gilbert *or* Sullivan operas, as well as the singers who appeared with Sullivan at the Leeds music festivals. This is followed by the singers who performed at the Savoy Theatre under Gilbert's direction in the 1906 to 1910 seasons. The final section of the discography gives details of the earliest attempts to record the complete operas.

The Gramophone Company began the manufacture of 7″* records in August of 1898. 10″ records were introduced in 1901 and were designated by the letters GC, for Gramophone Concert record, preceding the catalogue number. 12″, or Gramophone Monarch records, were introduced in 1903, and were designated by a catalogue number beginning with 0. The manufacture of 7″ records was discontinued in 1906.

Catalogue numbers are listed to the left of the record titles, and matrix numbers appear to the right. Catalogue numbers to the right, preceded by the letters B, C, D, or E are later re-issues on double-sided discs. All Gramophone recordings listed here were issued in single-sided form prior to World War I; all Odeon Company recordings were double-sided. All records listed in this discography were made by the Gramophone Company unless otherwise indicated. The trade mark 'His Masters Voice' was introduced on the record labels in February 1909.

No matrix numbers were assigned to the earliest series of Gramophone Company records, begun in August of 1898. In early November, 1898 an unlettered matrix number was assigned to every 'take' of every selection recorded. In May of 1901 various letters began to appear before and after the Company's matrix numbers. The suffix letters to Gramophone Company matrix numbers which appear in this book indicate the following:

*The abbreviation ″ for inches will be used throughout the book.

| a, b, c | a 7″, 10″ or 12″ record taken by Fred Gaisberg |
| d, e, f | a 7″, 10″ or 12″ record taken by Will Gaisberg |
| g, h, i | a 7″, 10″ or 12″ record taken by the engineer W. Sinkler Darby |
| B | an early 7″ record taken by W. Sinkler Darby |
| D, XD | a record taken by W. Sinkler Darby |
| R | a record taken by the engineer Bedford Royal [usually 12″] |
| ab, af | a later series of 10″ records |
| ac, ag | a later series of 12″ records |
| FG, G | a record taken by Fred Gaisberg |
| W | a record taken by Will Gaisberg |
| z, A | an early 7″ or 10″ record recorded on the Continent |

The prefix letters to matrix numbers indicate the following:

| WCG | a record taken by Will Gaisberg |
| Ho | a new series of records begun in 1912 |
| AC | a 12″ record taken by the engineer Hancox |
| nB | a record made by the new 'all wax' process begun May, 1901 [This designation was soon dropped] |

The prefix Lx appearing before a matrix number indicates merely that the record was on the Odeon label. Matrix references Ab or y indicate that the record was on the Zonophone label, and matrix prefixes A, AX and WAX indicate that the record was a Columbia.

Matrix suffixes X, or -1, -2, etc. indicate alternate takes of the same record.

The letters CR indicate that the singer created the role on the recording in the British première of the opera or musical.

Details of all the known records are given for all singers included in this discography with the exception of David Bispham, John Coates, Ben Davies, George Grossmith, Jr., Julius Lieban, Harold Wilde, Ellen Beach Yaw, and the singers who worked with Sullivan at Leeds. These are artists who were not known for their singing of Gilbert and Sullivan, and who made large numbers of recordings which, for the purpose of this survey, are irrelevant.

Most of the important recordings in this book have been re-issued by Pearl Records and are available on LP. These records are listed in the final section of the book.

This discography would not have been possible without the indefatigible assistance of Leonard Petts who researched hundreds of matrix numbers, told me of many records I had not known of, and painstakingly corrected many errors.

I am also grateful to the Beinecke Rare Book and Manuscript Library at Yale University for permission to quote from Arthur Sullivan's private diaries. I am grateful as well to Michael Walters and Peter Adamson who supplied me with much needed additional information.

*John Wolfson*

# INTRODUCTION

Sometime in 1894 Emile Berliner, a German inventor living in America, perfected the technique of recording on a flat disc. In 1895 the US Gramophone Co. was incorporated. Late the same year a motor was developed to keep the record turntable revolving at a constant speed, and in 1897, the first American recording studio was opened in Philadelphia. The following year, Fred Gaisberg, the world's first 'A and R' man, was chosen to establish the first recording studio in London for the European branch of the Gramophone Company.

When Gaisberg arrived in London in the summer of 1898, Gilbert and Sullivan were still alive, their operas were still being performed at the Savoy, and every major star of the Savoy Theatre (except for Jessie Bond who had retired to get married two years earlier) was alive and well and working in or near London.

In August 1898, when the Gramophone Company began recording, a revival of *The Gondoliers* was playing at the Savoy with a cast that included Henry Lytton, Walter Passmore, Robert Evett, Rosina Brandram, Blanche Gaston Murray, Isabel Jay and Ruth Vincent. A few blocks away at the Prince of Wales Theatre, Courtice Pounds was starring in an adaptation of *La Poupée* by Audran, then in the eighteenth month of its run. Rutland Barrington had just opened as Marcus Pomponius in George Edwardes' production of *A Greek Slave* at Daly's. Richard Temple was about to go into rehearsal for *The Sorcerer* which would open at the Savoy the following month. George Grossmith was in rehearsal with his brother Weedon for a farce comedy called *Young Mr. Yarde* for which he had written the music. Within the next ten years all of these artists (except unfortunately George Grossmith and Rosina Brandram) would stand before the recording horn.

Fred Gaisberg set up the first European studio of the Gramophone Company in the basement of Number 31, Maiden Lane, two doors away from Rule's Restaurant, which was, at the turn of the century a popular gathering spot for theatrical performers. The gramophone was quite unknown in London when Fred Gaisberg arrived, and consequently in the earliest days of the Gramophone Company Mr Gaisberg and his staff were not above dropping into the bar at Rule's, where they would run into this or that performer 'accidentally'. The performer would then be invited back to the recording studio for a demonstration of the wonderful new invention. In this way, a large number of singers were first introduced to the talking machine.

Marching bands and 'singers who were loud' recorded best on the primitive recording equipment. Cornets and tenors were reproduced to greatest advantage and the recording world became divided for acoustic purposes into two kinds of people: those whose voices recorded well, and those whose did not.

One singer whose voice did record well on the nineteenth century equipment, and who is now remembered as a pioneer recording artist, was a young tenor named Scott Russell. He had appeared in the premières of *Utopia, (Limited)* and *The Grand Duke*. When Gaisberg met him in 1898 he was appearing with Rutland Barrington in *A Greek Slave* at Daly's Theatre, off Leicester Square, just a few minutes from Maiden Lane. Scott Russell made his first recordings in August, 1898, only two weeks after the Gramophone Company had begun recording. One of the first songs he recorded was 'Take a Pair of Sparkling Eyes' from *The Gondoliers*.

In December of 1899 Fred Gaisberg returned to America for a holiday. On the boat back to England, he met Edna May, the star of *An American Beauty* which was soon to open in London. After the show's première, Miss May appeared in the recording studios in Maiden Lane to make three of the earliest 'original cast' recordings.

Late in 1900, however, a more organized experiment was made in the field of original cast recordings when singers from three current shows were invited to the studios. The musicals to be recorded were *San Toy* (5 records), *Florodora* (14 records), and *Patience* (3 records), the last constituting the first recordings by the D'Oyly Carte Opera Company.

The studios in Maiden Lane were not more than a five-minute walk from the Savoy, and on 19 December 1900, Walter Passmore, some time before his evening performance, stopped by and recorded two songs, 'If You're Anxious for to Shine' from *Patience* and 'My Name is John Wellington Wells' from *The Sorcerer* in which he had appeared two years before. The following day, members of the Savoy Opera Chorus recorded two more excerpts from *Patience* and one from *The Pirates of Penzance*, the latter with Isabel Jay. Two weeks later, Henry Lytton made the first of his many solo visits to the studios and the first of his many recordings of 'The Laughing Song'.

And that was how it began. By the beginning of 1901, after a year and a half of very primitive operation, the Gramophone Company had succeeded in recording Henry Lytton, Walter Passmore, Isabel Jay and the D'Oyly Carte Opera Company Chorus, all within a two week period.

Later in 1901, the first 10" records were released. In 1902 Richard Temple began to record. In 1903 the first 12" records were released, and on one of them a Henry Lytton creator's (CR) record from *A Princess of Kensington*. In 1904 the first double-sided records appeared. In 1905 Rutland Barrington made his one and only recording on cylinder, and in 1906 Robert Evett became a recording artist. 1907 saw the release of the first (almost) complete Gilbert and Sullivan recording, *The Yeoman of the Guard* on Pathé, and in 1908, ten years after the beginning of commercial recording in London, a complete recording of *The Mikado* was issued by the Odeon Company with Walter Passmore – the first complete recording of a Gilbert and Sullivan opera with an original Savoyard in the cast. *The Savoyards on Record* tells the story of these records and the artists who made them.

Arthur Sullivan.

## SIR ARTHUR SULLIVAN

One of the most unusual documents of recorded sound to survive, and appropriately enough, the earliest in this collection, is the voice of Arthur Sullivan.

Thomas Edison built his first tin foil phonograph in 1877. He then put his "favorite invention" aside for several years, to work on the electric light. He returned to the phonograph in the 1880s and by 1888 had developed a working model. He built a number of them which he sent to Europe with his own representatives whose instructions were simply to record the voices of as many famous people as they possibly could.

The man sent by Edison to England was one Col. Gouraud. With an invention as impressive as the phonograph, the Colonel had little trouble in getting himself invited to the homes of fashionable Londoners – Alfred Rothschild among others – where, after dinner, he would first demonstrate the invention, and then invite some of the guests to talk into the machine. In this way he recorded the voices of Browning, Tennyson, Florence Nightingale, the Duke of Cambridge, and many more.

On 5 October 1888, five days after the opening of *The Yeomen of the Guard*, Arthur Sullivan, in an outspoken mood, recorded the following message to Thomas Edison, ten years before the beginning of commercial recording in London:

> Dear Mr. Edison,
>
> For myself, I can only say that I am astonished and somewhat terrified at the result of this evening's experiment – astonished at the wonderful form you have developed, and terrified at the thought that so much hideous and bad music will be put on record forever.
>
> But all the same, I think it is the most wonderful thing that I have ever experienced and I congratulate you with all my heart on this wonderful discovery.
>
> Arthur Sullivan

Rutland Barrington in *The Geisha*.

# RUTLAND BARRINGTON

Rutland Barrington (1853-1922) was only twenty-four years old when Mrs Howard Paul, the original Lady Sangazure, recommended him for a role in *The Sorcerer*. He subsequently played leading roles in all of the Gilbert and Sullivan operas up to and including *The Grand Duke*. While his greatest success was his characterization of Pooh-Bah, he created a few lighter roles as well, Captain Corcoran, Grosvenor, and Giuseppe. He was on leave of absence from the Savoy during the original production of *The Yeomen of the Guard*, and did not appear as Wilfred Shadbolt until the revival of 1907. He first played the Grand Inquisitor in *The Gondoliers* in 1908. During the famous 'carpet quarrel' he appeared in *Haddon Hall* for Sullivan and *His Excellency* for Gilbert.

After 1896 he appeared primarily in musical comedies, including such notable successes as *The Geisha, San Toy, A Country Girl*, and *The Cingalee*. He appeared as Falstaff in *The Merry Wives of Windsor* at a gala at His Majesty's in 1911, and as Polonius in *Hamlet* and Christopher Sly in *The Taming of the Shrew* at the same theatre in 1916. He was seldom out of work until his retirement due to illness in 1919. A benefit was held for him at the Savoy a few months before his death.

In the beginning of 1905 Barrington appeared on a Variety Bill at the Coliseum. One of the songs in his act was *The Moody Mariner*, the only song he ever recorded. Although it is only on a two-minute cylinder, the recording is successful enough to solve many riddles. Barrington's singing is laconic and employs much parlando. The ease with which he achieves an air of urbane superiority is quite marvellous. His style has surprising similarities to that of Walter Passmore, who was generally regarded as George Grossmith's successor. It is well to remember, however, that Gilbert asked Passmore to play the Sergeant of Police and the Grand Inquisitor, two roles which Barrington played at one time or another. Barrington's delivery is also reminiscent of Leo Sheffield, another artist who worked with Gilbert and succeeded to many of Barrington's roles.

The Barrington cylinder suggests that the Walter Passmore and Leo Sheffield recordings of Barrington's roles may be as close as we can ever get to what Gilbert actually had in mind.

**Edison Bell Cylinder, 1905**

6630          'The Moody Mariner'

## RICHARD TEMPLE

Richard Temple (1847-1912) was born Richard Barker Cobb, and made
his debut at the Crystal Palace in 1872. He created the role of Sir
Marmaduke in *The Sorcerer* at the Opera Comique in 1877 and thereafter
appeared in the premières of all of the Gilbert and Sullivan operas through
*The Yeomen of the Guard.* With the exception of *Iolanthe,* in which he
played Strephon, he created the leading bass roles. In 1890 he toured as
Giuseppe in *The Gondoliers,* a role he never played in London. He
continued to appear in these roles in revivals at the Savoy until 1908. He
also played in *Princess Toto* (Gilbert and Clay) and *The Chieftain* (Sullivan
and Burnand). He sang Rigoletto at the beginning of his career. He played
in a few West End musicals in the 1890s, including *Morocco Bound* (music
by Osmond Carr).

He became a teacher at the Royal College of Music where George Baker
met him. He directed many student productions with C.V. Stanford
conducting, including *Falstaff, Dido and Aeneas,* and the famous
production of *Orfeo* which featured Clara Butt.

Richard Temple's records are notoriously rare with only one or two copies of each known to exist. The unissued recording from *The Marriage of Figaro* is sung in an archaic English translation. Temple employs an unusual candenza which, curiously enough, was also recorded by Charles Sentley and Peter Dawson. Temple's recording had a catalogue number assigned to it (and for this reason it has survived in a test pressing) but it was never issued. Not long after this recording was made, Charles Santley recorded the same aria in Italian which quite possibly is the reason why the Temple record was withdrawn.

### Black G & T, 22 October 1902

| | | |
|---|---|---|
| unissued | *The Mikado*. 'The Mikado's Song' | 2604b |
| GC2-2767 | *The Mikado*. 'The Mikado's Song' | 2605b |
| unissued | *The Pirates of Penzance*. 'I am a Pirate King' | 2606b |

[Matrix numbers 2603b and 2607b are unknown and may also be by Richard Temple.]

### (?) April 1903

| | | |
|---|---|---|
| 02016 | 'I am a Friar of Orders Grey' | 78R |
| | | (later C) |

### 13 May 1903

| | | |
|---|---|---|
| GC2-2928 | *The Pirates of Penzance*. 'I am a Pirate King' | 3669b |
| unissued | *A Masked Ball*. 'Eri Tu' | 3670b |
| [GC2-2972] | *The Marriage of Figaro*. | 3672b |
| | 'Go to Bed, your Vagaries are Over' [Non Piu Andrai] | |

[Matrix number 3671b is unknown and may also be by Richard Temple.]

10″ Black Label G & T, 1903.

# AMY AUGARDE

Amy Augarde (1868-1959) made her début in the D'Oyly Carte chorus in 1884. She became Jessie Bond's understudy, played Cousin Hebe in the 1888 revival of *H.M.S. Pinafore* and appeared as Mad Margaret when Miss Bond was taken ill shortly after the opening of *Ruddigore*.

On leaving the Savoy, she appeared in *Doris* and *Dorothy* by Alfred Cellier, and later in *The Little Michus* (with Isabel Jay), *The Chocolate Soldier* (with Charles Workman), and *A Waltz Dream* (with Robert Evett). She was seldom out of work during a career that lasted over fifty years. One of the last things she appeared in was the revival of *The Rose of Persia* in 1935.

While she appeared at the Savoy as a soubrette, her only Gilbert and Sullivan recordings (made twenty years later) are of contralto roles, which she sang very effectively.

**Black G & T, 15 August 1906**

| | | |
|---|---|---|
| GC3-2468 | 'Laughs I have Met' (w. Maurice Farkoa, et al) | 8659b |
| unissued | 'The Murder of Rizzio' (w. Albert Whelan) | 8656-8b |

**28 August 1906**

| | | |
|---|---|---|
| unissued | *The Mikado.* Solo and recit. (presumably 'Alone and Yet Alive') | 8789-90b |

**1 November 1906**

| | | |
|---|---|---|
| GC1326 | 'Darby and Joan's Christmas' (w. Albert Whelan)* | 4789h |
| unissued | *The Mikado.* 'Alone and Yet Alive' | 4791h |
| unissued | 'Ora Pro Nobis' (Piccolomini) | 4792h |

*Also issued on Zono T6052 and T267

**Zonophone, 1908**

| | | |
|---|---|---|
| X44085 | 'I Surrender All' (w. Deering, Pike, Dawson, Clifford) | 8804e |
| X44088 | 'Christ Arose' (w. Deering, Pike, Dawson, Stewart) | 8806e |

['Deering' on the above two records is Eleanor Jones Hudson.]

**Winner Records**

| | |
|---|---|
| 2436 | *The Mikado.* 'Madrigal' (w. Elda May, Wilfred Virgo, Robert Carr) |
| 2437 | *The Mikado.* 'There is Beauty in the Bellow of the Blast' (w. Robert Carr) |
| 2437 | *The Mikado.* 'Were You not to Ko-ko Plighted' (w. Wilfred Virgo) |

See Complete Recordings: *H.M.S. Pinafore* [Gramophone Company, 1908]
*The Mikado* [Gramophone Company, 1906]

**Odeon, 1911**

| | | |
|---|---|---|
| 0705 | *The Chocolate Soldier.* 'Tale of a Coat' (w. Ch. Workman et al) | Lx3531 |
| 0703 | *The Chocolate Soldier.* Finale, Act II (w. Ch. Workman et al) | Lx3532 |

**Columbia, 1915**

| | | |
|---|---|---|
| 2596 | *Shell Out.* 'Girls, Girls, Girls' | 29961 |

**Columbia, 1920**

| | | |
|---|---|---|
| F1066 | *The Naughty Princess.* 'Great Great Grandmother' (w. Lily St. John) | 74206-2 |
| F1066 | *The Naughty Princess.* 'Etiquette' (w. Lily St. John, George Grossmith) | 74207-2 |
| unissued | *The Naughty Princess.* 'Years Ago'/'Cock-a-doodle-doo' | 74205-1-2 |

## BILLIE BARLOW

Billie Barlow (1862-1937) made her début at the Opera Comique in
*H.M.S. Pinafore* under her real name, Minnie Barlow. It was W.S. Gilbert
who suggested that she change it to Billie.

She went to New York with the D'Oyly Carte Company in 1879 where
she appeared as Isabel in the première of *The Pirates of Penzance*. She was in
the London production of *Patience* in 1881, but that marked the end of
her career in Gilbert and Sullivan. She went back to America where she
spent the next four years touring in operetta. When she returned to
England, she played Nellie Farren's part in *Monte Cristo, Jun.*

In 1888 she began to appear in the Music Halls and in Variety. She is
better remembered for this part of her career. Two of her most successful
turns were 'See Me Dance the Polka' and 'It's English, Quite English, You
Know'. Later she spent several years touring Australia and South Africa
where she appeared in English musical comedies as well as the Music
Halls.

Her recordings are all taken from her Music Hall repertoire.

### 28 June 1903

| | | | |
|---|---|---|---|
| 03031 | 'Mashing the Band' | 213C | |
| GC3455 | 'I'm Not Supposed to Know' | 3943R | (later b) |
| GC3456 | 'How to Sing a Song' | 3946R | (later b) |
| Zon X-43041 | 'Lady Barber' | 3945R | (later b) |
| unissued | 'How to Sing a Song' | 3942R | (later b) |
| unissued | 'It Does Go' | 3944R | (later b) |

# LOUIE HENRI

Louie Henri made her stage début in 1882. She was appearing with Kate
Santley's company in 1883 when Henry Lytton joined. They were married
in 1884, the year in which they first appeared with the D'Oyly Carte
Company. She and her husband toured with the company from 1888 to
1896, during which time Miss Henri played all the soubrette roles as well as
Julia Jellicoe in *The Grand Duke*. In 1891 she played Tessa in the revival of
*The Gondoliers* in London. It was her only appearance at the Savoy. After
that she retired from the stage to devote herself to her family. Some years
later, she appeared in silent films.

c. March 1902

| | | | |
|---|---|---|---|
| 4160 | 'Old Daddy Long Legs' (w. Lytton) | | 1601b |

c. June 1902

| | | | |
|---|---|---|---|
| 3247 | A *Country Girl*. 'Under the Deeodar' | | 4641 nB (later a) |
| 4062 | A *Country Girl*. 'Two Little Chicks' (w. Lytton) | | 4668a |
| 4084 | A *Country Girl*. 'Quarrelling' (w. Lytton) | | 4669a |
| GC4161 | *Iolanthe*. 'None Shall Part Us' (w. Lytton) | | 1986b |

April 16 1903

| | | | |
|---|---|---|---|
| unissued | *The Girl from Kay's*. 'Coon Song' | (10") | 3475b |

April 24 1903

| | | | |
|---|---|---|---|
| GC4243 | *The Girl from Kay's*. 'Semi-Detatched' (w. Lytton) | | 3520b |
| GC4336 | *The Girl from Kay's*. 'Make It Up' (w. Lytton) | | 3521b |
| GC4244 | A *Country Girl*. 'Two Little Chicks' (w. Lytton) | | 3522b |
| GC4245 | A *Country Girl*. 'Quarrelling' (w. Lytton) | | 3523b |
| unissued | *The Girl from Kay's*. 'Semi-Detached' (w. Lytton) | (7") | 5305a |
| 4295 | *The Girl from Kay's*. 'Make it Up' (w. Lytton) | | 5306a |

Records with suffix letter 'a' are 7"; records with suffix letter 'b' are 10".

The young Henry Lytton in *Iolanthe*.

## HENRY LYTTON

Henry A. Lytton (1860-1936) was a member of the D'Oyly Carte Company almost continuously for fifty years. He first appeared in the chorus of a touring company of *Princess Ida* in which he understudied King Gama. In 1888 he earned the admiration of Gilbert when he replaced George Grossmith on short notice for a few performances of *Ruddigore* at the Savoy. Thereafter he appeared in every conceivable type of part: light baritone (Strephon, Dr. Daly), bass (the Mikado, the Pirate King), as well as the principal comedy roles for which he is remembered.

He spent a few seasons (1903-1906) in musical comedy in the West End, and appeared in *The Earl and the Girl*, *The Talk of The Town*, and *The White Chrysanthemum*. He returned to the D'Oyly Carte Company at Gilbert's invitation in 1907, and was its principal comedian from 1909 until his retirement in 1934. His last stage appearance was as the King of China in *Aladdin* in December of that year.

Henry Lytton had a most unusual recording career, which fell conveniently into two phases, 1901-5 and 1925-32. In the early period he recorded songs from West End musicals and excerpts from the Savoy Operas in which he was appearing as a young man, generally as the romantic lead. In the later phase, he recorded four of the principal comedy roles. It is a great pity that the Gramophone Company considered him 'too old' in the 1920s to record the Lord Chancellor, John Wellington Wells, and the rest of the roles which he was still playing on stage.

Lytton wrote a Variety number called 'The Laughing Song' which he recorded at least seven times.

In the following list, a suffix letter 'a' following a matrix number indicates a 7" record; a suffix letter 'b' indicates a 10" record.

### 2 January 1901

| | | |
|---|---|---|
| 2277 | 'The Laughing Song' | 1890D |
| | | (later a) |

### c. March 1902

| | | |
|---|---|---|
| 4160 | 'Old Daddy Long Legs' (w. Louie Henri) | 1601b |

### April 1902

| | | |
|---|---|---|
| GC2-2654 | Merrie England. 'The Yeoman of England'  CR  (10") | 1908b |

### May 1902

| | | |
|---|---|---|
| 2-2103 | 'The Curate's Song' | 4583FG |
| | | (later a) |
| 2-2104 | 'You'd Better Ask Me' (Lohr) | 4581a |
| 2-2105 | 'The Laughing Song' | 4580a |
| 2-2110 | The Toreador. 'Everybody's Awfully Good to Me' | 4625G |
| | | (later a) |
| | also pressed from | 4626W |
| | | (later a) |
| 2-2111 | The Country Girl. 'Peace, Peace' | 4624W |
| | | (later a) |
| 2-2112 | The Toreador. 'When I Marry Amelia' | 4627G |
| | | (later a) |
| 2-2113 | Prince Methuselam. 'The Dotlet of My Eye' | |
| | (trans. Arthur Roberts) | 4629a |

### June 1902

| | | |
|---|---|---|
| 2-2125 | Merrie England. 'Imagination' | 4672G |
| | | (later a) |
| 2-2136 | A Country Girl. 'Me and Mrs. Brown' | 4670a |
| 2-2137 | The Toreador. 'Archie, Archie' | 4671a |
| 4062 | A Country Girl. 'Two Little Chicks' (w. Louie Henri) | 4668a |
| 4084 | A Country Girl. 'Quarrelling' (w. Louie Henri) | 4669a |
| GC4161 | Iolanthe. 'None Shall Part Us' (w. Louie Henri)  (10") | 1986b |

(continued over)

**Henry Lytton (cont.)**               **30 August 1902**
2-2148                   'The Laughing Song'                                    4923D
                         [Promotional record for *Pearson's Weekly*]            (later a)
unissued                 *The Messenger Boy.* 'When the Boys Come Home'         4924X

### 16 April 1903
unissued                 'He Was a Sailor'                          (10″)    3473-4b
unissued                 'The Laughing Song'                        (10″)    3476-7b*

*Louie Henri's unissued recording of 'The Coon Song' was mat. 3475b

### 24 April 1903
GC4243                   *The Girl from Kay's.* 'Semi-Detached' (w. Louie Henri)      3520b
GC4336                   *The Girl from Kay's.* 'Make it Up' (w. Louie Henri)         3521b
GC4244                   *A Country Girl.* 'Two Little Chicks' (w. Louie Henri)       3522b
GC4245                   *A Country Girl.* 'Quarrelling' (w. Louie Henri)             3523b
unissued                 *A Princess of Kensington.* 'Four Jolly Sailormen'          3524b
                         ["Savoy Theatre Male Quartet" acc. to label]
GC4246                   *A Princess of Kensington.* 'Four Jolly Sailormen'          3525b
                         ["Savoy Theatre Male Quartet" acc. to label]
04000                    *A Princess of Kensington.* 'Four Jolly Sailormen'   (12″)    86R
                         ["Savoy Theatre Male Quartet" acc. to label]
unissued                 *The Girl from Kay's.* 'Semi-Detached' (w. Louie Henri)      5305a
4295                     *The Girl from Kay's.* 'Make it Up' (w. Louie Henri)         5306a

### 14 April 1904
unissued                 *The Earl and the Girl.* 'My Cosy Corner Girl'       CR   5179-80b
unissued                 *The Earl and the Girl.*                             CR       5181b
                         'By the Shore of the Mediterranean'
unissued                 *The Earl and the Girl.* 'My Cosy Corner Girl'       CR       6128a
unissued                 *The Earl and the Girl.*                             CR       6130a
                         'By the Shore of the Mediterranean'
unissued                 'The Laughing Song'                                           6129a

### 21 April 1904
GC3 2072                 *The Earl and the Girl.* 'My Cosy Corner Girl'       CR      5232b*
unissued                 *The Earl and the Girl.* 'My Cosy Corner Girl'       CR       5231b
GC3 2079                 *The Earl and the Girl.*                             CR       5233b
                         'By the Shore of the Mediterranean'
2-2462                   *The Earl and the Girl.* 'My Cosy Corner Girl'                6166a
2-2463                   *The Earl and the Girl.*                             CR       6167a
                         'By the Shore of the Mediterranean'
                         Isabel Jay recorded matrix numbers 5227-30b

### 19 June 1905 (10″)
Zon X42329               'He Was a Sailor'                                             2176e
GC3-2300                 'The Laughing Song'                                           2177e
unissued                 *Iolanthe.* 'Dream Song' [e.g., 'The Nightmare Song']         2175e

**Edison Bell Cylinders, 1905**

| 6941 | 'The Laughing Song' |
| 6842 | 'You Can't Please Everybody Always' |
| 6843 | 'The Vicar's Song' [Probably from *The Sorcerer*] |

**Musogram (11½")**

| 98 | 'The Laughing Song' ['Hill-and-Dale', edge start] |

**12 July 1911 (10")**

| GC4-2153 | 'The Laughing Song' (w. orchestra) | B453 | 13767e |

**HMV Test Pressings, November 1919 (10")**

| unissued | *The Gondoliers.* 'In Enterprise of Martial Kind' | Ho | 5409 ae |
| unissued | *The Yeomen of the Guard.* 'I've Jibe and Joke' | Ho | 5410 ae |

Henry Lytton appeared in the following complete recordings for the Gramophone Company

| 1925 | *Princess Ida.* King Gama |
| 1926 | *The Mikado.* Ko-Ko |
| 1927 | *The Gondoliers.* Duke of Plaza-Toro |
| 1930 | *H.M.S. Pinafore.* Sir Joseph |
| 1932 | *Princess Ida.* King Gama |

See Complete Recordings, p. 90

7" Berliner with raised lettering, 1902.

## J.G. ROBERTSON

J.G. [Jack] Robertson was born in Peru. He came to England to study at the Royal Academy of Music. He made his début in Henry Irving's production of *Much Ado About Nothing* at the Lyceum in 1882. In that production he sang 'Sigh No More, Ladies.' Clement Scott, the drama critic, wrote that Robertson had "not only a sweet and expressive voice, but well understood the grace and delicacy of this charming lyric. He did not come down to the footlights and deliver his song in a full bodied way as operatic tenors are wont to do, but he acted Balthasaar and belonged to the scene." It is easy to see how Robertson would have been popular with W.S. Gilbert, who tended to dislike tenors.

J.G. Robertson was the principal tenor at the Savoy during the 1887-8 season. He appeared, however, only in revivals: *H.M.S. Pinafore, The Pirates of Penzance,* and *The Mikado,* filling the gap between the departure of Durward Lely at the close of *Ruddigore* and the arrival of Courtice Pounds at the beginning of *The Yeomen of the Guard.* In 1893 Gilbert cast him as Alfredo, the leading tenor in *The Mountebanks.*

Robertson appeared in a few unsuccessful West End musicals in the nineties. By the turn of the century he had become a successful concert singer.

**30 January 1899 (7")**

2357                        *Much Ado About Nothing.* 'Sigh No More, Ladies'                        1117
(unlettered series)

**11 June 1915**

The Gramophone Company made two test pressings by a singer named Jack Robertson. It is not possible, however, to say whether this was the same J.G. Robertson of the Savoy.

'Those Azure Eyes' (Cox)                                        Ho1541
'Eyes that Used to Gaze into Mine' (Lohr)                        Ho1542

# COURTICE POUNDS

Charles Courtice Pounds (1862-1927) claimed in an early issue of *The Green Room* to have made his début in the original production of *Patience* as understudy to Durward Lely (the Duke) *and* Rutland Barrington (Grosvenor)! This was the beginning of a long career in the musical theatre. He played leads in West End productions for forty years.

Courtice Pounds was principal tenor in the American productions of *Princess Ida*, *The Mikado*, and *Ruddigore*. He returned to England to appear in the premières of *The Yeomen of the Guard* and *The Gondoliers* at the Savoy. Like Durward Lely, he was admired by Gilbert as a "tenor who could act", a fact borne out by his recordings. He remained at the Savoy to appear in *Haddon Hall* and *The Chieftain*.

After leaving the D'Oyly Carte Company in 1894, he appeared in such West End successes as *La Poupée*, *The Belle of Mayfair*, and *Princess Caprice*. He played the tenor lead in *Chu Chin Chou* at His Majesty's Theatre for five years and appeared in *The Boatswain's Mate* by Dame Ethel Smyth. He was a versatile performer, and once played Touchstone in *As You Like It* at the Haymarket. Thirty-five years after his Savoy successes, he starred as Franz Schubert in *Lilac Time*.

It is lamentable that his only Gilbert and Sullivan recording was unissued.

### HMV, 1916

| | | | | |
|---|---|---|---|---|
| 02659 | *My Lady Frayle.* | | | |
| | 'Song of the Bowl' | CR 4/16 | | Ho1772ac |
| 02668 | 'Come into the Garden, Maud' | 5/16 | D446 | Ho1818ac |
| unissued | *The Yeomen of the Guard.* 'Is Life a Boon?' | | | Ho2821ab |
| 02697 | *The Boatswain's Mate.* | | | |
| | 'When Rocked in the Billows' | CR 2/10/16 | D446 | Ho2189af |
| 04184 | *The Boatswain's Mate.* | | | |
| | 'The First Thing To Do' | CR | | |
| | (w. Rosina Buckman, Frederick Ranalow) | 2/10/16 | D447 | Ho2192-3af |
| 04186 | *Chu Chin Chow.* | | | |
| | 'Any Time's Kissing Time' | CR | | |
| | (w. Violet Essex) | 11/16 | D417 | Ho2330af |
| GC4-2812 | *Chu Chin Chow.* | | | |
| | 'When a Pullet is Plump' | CR 11/16 | E172 | Ho3317ae |

### Vocalion, 1923

| | | | |
|---|---|---|---|
| | From *Lilac Time:* | | |
| K05065 | 'The Golden Song' (w. Clara Butterworth) | CR | 03151 |
| K05065 | 'Underneath the Lilac Bough' [Quintet] | CR | 03149-x |
| K05067 | 'Dream Enthralling' | CR | 03150 |
| K05067 | 'Dear Flower, Small and Wise' | | |
| | (w. Clara Butterworth) | CR | 03153-x |

## ESTHER PALLISER

Esther Palliser was born to a musical family in Philadelphia. She studied on the Continent with Mme Viardot Garcia and Mme Marchesi, through the last of whom she probably met Sullivan. Esther Palliser appeared in *Ivanhoe* and *Haddon Hall*. In the New York production of *The Gondoliers* she played Gianetta, a role in which she occasionally appeared at the Savoy. She sang for three seasons at Covent Garden where, in addition to playing Santuzza and Brangaene, she alternated with Nellie Melba in *Faust*. She sang in *Alexander's Feast* by Handel and Bach's B Minor Mass, both conducted by Sullivan at the Leeds Festival in 1898. All of her recordings are very rare.

### Black G & T, 1902

| | | |
|---|---|---|
| GC3288 | 'Spring' (Tosti) | 2100b |
| GC3289 | 'The Sweetest Flower that Blows' | 2101b |
| GC3290 | 'La Foletta' (Marchesi) | 2102b |

### 2 September 1902

| | | |
|---|---|---|
| GC4179 | 'Bolero' (Saint-Saëns) (w. May Walters Palliser) | 2256b |
| unissued | 'Bolero' (Saint-Saëns) (w. May Walters Palliser) | 2255b |
| unissued | 'The Lark Now Leaves' (w. May Walters Palliser) | 2257b |
| unissued | 'La Foletta' (w. May Walters Palliser) | 2258b |
| unissued | 'Nocturne' (Chaminade) (w. May Walters Palliser) | 2259-60b |

### 4 November 1902

| | | | |
|---|---|---|---|
| 53243 | *Xerxes.* 'Largo' | | 2671b |
| unissued | *Xerxes.* 'Largo' | | 2670b |
| GC3288X | 'Spring' (Tosti) | | 2673b |
| unissued | 'Spring' (Tosti) | | 2672b |
| unissued | 'The Guardian Angel' (Liza Lehmann) | (7″) | 5150a |

Walter Passmore in *The Sorcerer*.

## WALTER PASSMORE

Walter Passmore (1867-1946) made his début at the Savoy Theatre in
*Jane Annie* in 1893, and was principal comedian there from 1894 to 1903.
He created the title role in *The Grand Duke* and appeared in *The Chieftain,*
*The Beauty Stone* and *The Rose of Persia.* Although Passmore was generally
regarded as George Grossmith's successor, Gilbert cast him as the Sergeant
of Police in *The Pirates of Penzance* and The Grand Inquisitor in *The
Gondoliers.*

Sullivan was fond of Passmore. After seeing him in *The Lucky Star* he
noted in his diary, "The fun of the whole piece lies in Passmore. Take him
out and nothing's left. He worked splendidly and carried the opera
through. I wish though he could drop his 'cockney' accent and manners at
times."

When the D'Oyly Carte Company left the Savoy to tour in 1903, Walter Passmore remained in London where he commenced a career in musical comedy which lasted twenty-five years. He appeared in such important West End productions as *The Earl and the Girl, The Talk of the Town* and *Madame Pompadour*. He was married to Agnes Fraser who frequently appeared with him on stage. During his legitimate stage career, however, he made only three recordings from the musical comedy repertoire, all from *The Talk of the Town* in 1905.

His theatrical performances were largely visual. George Baker remembers his Sergeant of Police as being "obstreperously funny". His singing of Ko-Ko in the Odeon *Mikado* in 1908 is probably his best recording. The Columbia records, issued about 1912 (no doubt as competition for the series which Charles Workman had recently made for Odeon) are less successful. In these, Passmore employs much parlando – possibly the result of his musical comedy technique – and his delivery sounds laconic to the modern listener. (Passmore's Columbias were recorded at speeds *above* 78 and they sound a bit less laconic when played up to pitch!).

Passmore created the role of Walter Wilkins in *Merrie England* in 1903. He toured in *Merrie England* in 1911, which is why he recorded three songs from the opera for Columbia. *The Big Brass Band* is his rarest record.

**19 December 1900 (7″)**

| | | |
|---|---|---|
| 2454 | *Patience.* 'Bunthorne's Song' | 1833a |
| 2455 | *The Sorcerer.* 'My Name is John Wellington Wells' | 1831a |

**Nicole, 1905 (10″)**

| | | |
|---|---|---|
| 5741 | *The Talk of the Town.* 'Bombay on the Nile' | CR |
| D565 | *The Talk of the Town.* 'If I were Vanderbuilt' | CR |
| D565 | *The Talk of the Town.* 'Me and my Little Brood' | CR |

See complete recordings: *The Mikado*, Odeon, 1908

**Columbia, 1912-13 (10″)**

| | | | |
|---|---|---|---|
| 1866 | *The Sorcerer.* 'My Name is John Wellington Wells' | | 27827 |
| 1866 | *The Pirates of Penzance.* 'The Policeman's Song' | | 27829 |
| 1818 | *The Gondoliers.* 'I Stole the Prince' | | 27830 |
| 1818 | *The Mikado.* 'The Flowers that Bloom in the Spring' | | 27831 |
| 2521* | *Merrie England.* 'The Big Brass Band' (w. Robert Howe) | CR | 28585-1-2 |
| 2521* | *Merrie England.* 'Imagination' | CR | 28588-1 |
| 2534* | *Patience.* 'When I Go Out of Door' (w. Robert Howe) | | 28586-2 |
| 2534* | *Patience.* 'Bunthorne's Song' (w. recit.) | | 28587-1.2 |

*These records were not issued until 1915.     **(continued over)**

**Walter Passmore (cont.)**

Columbia, 1912-13 (12″)

| | | | |
|---|---|---|---|
| 317 | *The Yeomen of the Guard.* | 6218 | |
| | 'Like a Ghost His Vigil Keeping' (w. Robert Howe) | | |
| 317 | *The Yeomen of the Guard.* 'I Have a Song to Sing Oh' | | 6220 |
| | (w. Hilda Francis) | | |
| 326 | *H.M.S. Pinafore.* 'When I was a Lad' | | 6219 |
| 326 | *The Mikado.* 'Tit Willow' | | 6221 |
| 354 | *The Yeomen of the Guard.* 'A Private Buffoon' | | 6263 |
| 354 | *Iolanthe.* 'Dream Song' [e.g. 'The Nightmare Song'] | | 6264 |
| 371 | *Trial by Jury.* 'The Judge's Song' | | 6313 |
| 371 | *Merrie England.* 'Fish Song' | CR | 6315 |
| 387 | *The Mikado.* 'The Criminal Cried' | | 6317 |
| | (w. Robert Howe, Carie Herwin) | | |
| 387 | *The Mikado.* 'Here's a How-de-do' | | 6318 |
| | (w. Robert Howe, Edward James) | | |

(Matrix numbers 6314 and 6316 are missing from the last session. There is no way of knowing whether Walter Passmore recorded any other titles at the time.)

Walter Passmore's first record, 1900.

Scott Russell as the Notary in *The Grand Duke*.

## SCOTT RUSSELL

H. Scott Russell (1868-1949) was a student of Gustave Garcia at the Royal
College of Music and made his London début in 1893 as Lord Dramaleigh
in *Utopia, (Limited)*. He then appeared in *Cox and Box*, *The Mikado*, *The
Yeomen of the Guard*, and *The Grand Duke*. He left the Savoy in 1897 to
appear in *A Greek Slave* at Daly's. He had a long career in musical comedy
and operetta in the West End, with appearances in *A Gaiety Girl*, *San Toy*,
*Veronique*, and *The Geisha*. He sang the leading tenor roles in the D'Oyly
Carte tour of 1902 and 1903, and appeared with the Beecham Light Opera
Company. After World War I he was with the Lyric Theatre
Hammersmith as actor and manager from 1920 to 1932. He retired in
1938.

Scott Russell was that rarest of singers, a tenor buffo, and his interpretation of 'A Tenor All Singers Above' and 'The Drinking Song' from *The Rose of Persia* give us some idea why Gilbert liked tenors who could act.

With the exception of two musical comedy roles in the 1920s, Scott Russell's recording career lasted from 1898 to 1901, when he made only seven-inch records, many of them with orchestral accompaniment! Although the orchestra did not replace the piano in the recording studio for several more years, an experiment with a small ensemble was made by the Gramophone Company for a few weeks in the autumn of 1900, during which time Scott Russell made many of his recordings. He was a pioneer recording artist. Few singers made as many records as he did in the early days, and few singers can be said to have virtually retired from making records as early as 1901!

All of the following are 7" Berliners!

### 19 August 1898

| | | | |
|---|---|---|---|
| E2005 | *The Geisha.* 'Jack's the Boy; | | |
| E2006 | *The Gondoliers.* 'Take a Pair of Sparkling Eyes' | | |
| E2007 | 'The Old Brigade' | | |

[The first day of commercial Gramophone recording in London was 2 August 1898. The three records listed above preceded the institution of serial matrix numbers.]

### 23 December 1898

| | | | |
|---|---|---|---|
| E2264 | 'Toast of the Dandy Fifth' | | 517 |

### 17 January 1899

| | | | |
|---|---|---|---|
| E2005X | *The Geisha.* 'Jack's the Boy' | | 905 |

### 18 January 1899

| | | | |
|---|---|---|---|
| E2338 | *A Greek Slave.* 'Saturnalia' | CR | 927 |

### 31 January 1899

| | | | |
|---|---|---|---|
| E2006X | *The Gondoliers.* 'Take a Pair of Sparkling Eyes' | | 1120 |
| E2007X | 'The Old Brigade' | | 1122 |

### 1 February 1899

| | | | |
|---|---|---|---|
| E2349 | 'Just One Girl' (Amy Williams, piano) | | 1130 |

[The above six records belong to the early 'unlettered' matrix series.]

### 21 November 1900

| | | | |
|---|---|---|---|
| 2963 | *The Rose of Persia.* 'Drinking Song' | | 1610a |
| 2970 | 'The Old Brigade' | | 1613a |
| 2972 | 'Marching to Pretoria' | | 1609a |
| 2973 | *Princess Ida.* 'Would You Know the Kind of Maid' | | 1611a |
| 2974 | *The Messenger Boy.* 'When the Boys Come Home' | | 1612a |
| 4082X | *San Toy.* 'When You are Wed to Me' (w. Miss Collier) | CR | 1618a |

### 26 November 1900

| | | | |
|---|---|---|---|
| 2971 | *Utopia, (Limited)*. 'A Tenor Can't Do Himself Justice' | | 1637a |
| 2983 | *The Geisha*. 'Jack's the Boy' | | 1639a |
| 2984 | *A Greek Slave*. 'The Girl of My Heart' | CR | 1641a |
| 2959 | *A Greek Slave*. 'The Revels' | CR | 1643a |

### 27 November 1900

| | | | |
|---|---|---|---|
| 2985 | *San Toy*. 'Love Has Come from Lotus Land' | CR | 1655a |
| 2960 | *San Toy*. 'The One in the World' | CR | 1654a |

### 19 December 1900

| | | | |
|---|---|---|---|
| 4078 | *San Toy*. 'Little Chinee Maid' (w. Miss Collier) | CR | 1842D(a) |

### 21 December 1900

| | | |
|---|---|---|
| 4046 | 'All's Well' (w. Ottley Cranston) | 1865D(a) |
| 4079 | *The Lily of Killarney*. 'The Moon Hath Raised her Lamp' (w. Ottley Cranston) | 1862D(a) |
| 4081 | 'Excelsior' (w. Ottley Cranston) | 1863D(a) |

### 26 February 1901

| | | |
|---|---|---|
| 4079X | *Lily of Killarney*. 'The Moon Hath Raised her Lamp' (w. Conway Dixon) | 2260a |

### 5 March 1901

| | | |
|---|---|---|
| 4046X | 'All's Well' (w. Conway Dixon) | 2336a |
| 4121 | 'Excelsior' (w. Conway Dixon) | 2335a |
| 4122 | 'Love and War' (w. Conway Dixon) | 2334a |
| 4123 | 'The Larboard Watch' (w. Conway Dixon) | 2333a |

Scott Russell also sang in the Lyric Hammersmith recordings of *The Beggar's Opera*, HMV D615 (1922) and *The Duenna*, Columbia, 9025-6 (1924).

## JOHN COATES

John Coates (1865-1941) began his career as a baritone. He appeared in the D'Oyly Carte Opera Chorus at the Savoy in 1893 and subsequently toured as Mr. Goldbury in *Utopia, (Limited)*. He played a few seasons of musical comedy and then decided to re-train his voice as a tenor.

It was during this period that he sang Sullivan's ballad 'The Absent-Minded Beggar' at a concert at the Alhambra with Sullivan conducting. The song had been written at the time of the Boer War to words by Kipling. [See page 74.]

Coates made his opera début as Claudio in Stanford's *Much Ado About Nothing* at Covent Garden in 1901. He appeared with the Moody Manners Opera Company in 1907-8 and sang Tristan and Siegfried for Beecham at Covent Garden in 1910-11. He had an extremely successful career in oratorio; he was Elgar's favourite Gerontius. After 1914 he specialized in Lieder.

John Coates had a long recording career which lasted well into the electric era. He made only one Gilbert and Sullivan recording, for three companies.

| | **G & T, 1907** | |
|---|---|---|
| GC3-2910 | *The Gondoliers*. 'Take a Pair of Sparkling Eyes' | 6730e |
| | **Pathé, c. 1912** | |
| 5054 | *The Gondoliers*. 'Take a Pair of Sparkling Eyes' | |
| | **Columbia, c. 1918** | |
| D1411 | *The Gondoliers*. 'Take a Pair of Sparkling Eyes' | 69257 |

---

## RUTH VINCENT

Ruth Vincent (1873-1936) made her début at the Savoy in *The Chieftain* in 1894. In the original production of *The Grand Duke* she was the understudy to Ilka von Palmay. The following year she replaced Mme Palmay as Elsie in *The Yeomen of the Guard*. Sullivan saw her in the Savoy production of *The Lucky Star* and noted in his diary, "Ruth Vincent looked as if she were furious at being relegated to the chorus."

The next production at the Savoy, however, was *The Gondoliers*, and Miss Vincent played Casilda. She had the lead in the ill-fated production of *The Beauty Stone*, and then played Aline in *The Sorcerer* and Josephine in *H.M.S. Pinafore*. This was followed by *The Rose of Persia*. When Miss

Vincent learned that there were to be *two* leading sopranos in the cast she was far from pleased, especially as the *other* soprano was the American, Ellen Beach Yaw, for whom Sullivan was writing special music. One week before the opening, Miss Vincent walked out! One of the few times anyone ever walked out at the Savoy. "Miss Vincent threw up her part, silly girl," Sullivan wrote in his diary [29 November 1899] "so we put Jessie Rose into it."

On leaving the Savoy, Ruth Vincent had a successful career in the West End, starring in *Veronique*, *Tom Jones* (by Edward German), and *The Belle of Brittany*. She then appeared with the Beecham Opera Company and at Covent Garden in *Hansel and Gretel*, *A Village Romeo and Juliet*, and *Carmen* (Michaela). In 1912 she began singing in oratorios and at Festivals. In the final phase of her career, she appeared at the Palladium and Variety Theatres.

### Columbia, 1906

| | | | |
|---|---|---|---|
| 3358 | 'Villanelle' (Dell 'Acqua) | (30001) | (A5014) |
| 3377 | 'Home Sweet Home' (Bishop) | (30002) | (A5009) |
| 30022 | 'Killarney' (Balfe) | | (A5020) |
| 30024 | 'Comin' Through the Rye' | | (A5021) |
| 30025 | 'Nymphs et Sylvains' (Bemberg) | | (A5016) |

### Columbia, 1908

| | | | |
|---|---|---|---|
| 6003 | *Amasis.* 'Little Prince, Look Up' (Faraday) | CR | |
| 6009 | *Tom Jones.* 'Waltz Song' (German) | CR | (A5086) |
| 6010 | 'Good-bye' (Tosti) | | |
| 6016 | *Il Penseroso.* 'Sweet Bird' (Handel) | | (A5086) |
| 6017 | *Pearl du Brasil.* 'Charmant Oiseau' (David) | | (A5077) |
| 6018 | 'Lo, Hear the Gentle Lark' (Bishop) | | (A5077) |

### HMV, 1904-1920

| | | | | |
|---|---|---|---|---|
| 2-3004 | 'A Birthday' (Cowen) | | E24 | y16647e |
| 2-3044 | 'I Wonder if Love is a Dream' (Forster) | | E25 | Ak18544e |
| 2-3049 | 'The Stars that Light My Garden' (Kennedy Russell) | | E26 | Ak18546e |
| 2-3069 | *Tom Jones.* Waltz Song (German) | CR | E27 | Ak18542e |
| 2-3289 | 'I Bring You Joy' (Haydn Wood) | | E25 | Ho3479ae |
| 2-3290 | 'In My Garden' (Liddle) | | E24 | Ho3480ae |
| 2-3418 | 'Three Roses' (Arden) | | E27 | Ho5289ae |
| 2-3269 | 'I Heard a Sweet Song' (Foster) [7/3/17] | | E26 | Ho3476ae |
| 03350 | 'Lilac Time' (Willeby) [4/6/13] | | D117 | Z7376f |
| 03520 | 'Love's Valley' (Forster) [26/7/16] | | | H02046af |
| 03566 | 'The Smile of Spring' (Fletcher) [3/17] | | D117 | Ho2509af |
| 2-053124 | 'Il Bacio' | | D113 | Ho1489ae |
| 03719 | 'Just a Little Waiting' (D. Wood) [26/9/19] | | D472 | Ho3979af |

Ilka von Palmay in *The Grand Duke*.

# ILKA von PALMAY

Mme Ilka von Palmay (1859-1945) was the Hungarian soprano whom Sullivan had to enjoin from appearing in the role of Nanki-Poo (!) in *The Mikado* in Germany in 1893\*. In 1895 she appeared with the Ducal Court Company of Saxe-Coburg and Gotha in five performances of *Der Vogelhändler* at Drury Lane. Gilbert saw her and hired her to play Julia Jellicoe in *The Grand Duke*, a role which he expanded considerably and tailored to her special talents. When she began her work at the Savoy, it surprised her to learn that no woman had ever appeared on that stage dressed as a man.

She had to sign a two-year contract with Richard D'Oyly Carte, and after *The Grand Duke* closed she appeared as Elsie in *The Yeomen of the Guard* in 1897. Sullivan, however, was not happy about her performance, and she was released from her contract and replaced by Ruth Vincent.

Her recordings, early Vienna and Budapest G & Ts, are virtually unknown in the English-speaking world. However, the few records she made in English and German display great charm and versatility, and it is easy to see why Gilbert liked her.

She was married to Count Kinsky and recorded under the name Ilka von Kinsky-Palmay. At the Savoy she appeared as Ilka von Palmay.

\*IREN SZEKELY, another Hungarian soprano actually recorded 'A Wand'ring Minstrel I' in Hungarian in 1905. It is an extraordinary example of a long past European tradition.

| | | |
|---|---|---|
| GC73236 | *Mikado*: 'Nanki-poo belépoje' | 6683b |
| | **Vienna, 1900 (7″)** | |
| 73002 | 'Ein Ungarisches Lied' (in Hungarian) | 1495A |
| 3195 | *The Circus Girl* 'A Little Piece of String' (in English) | 1496A |
| | **Budapest, 1903 (7″)** | |
| 73037 | 'Rupi, rupi' and 'Jer szivemre tubiczám' folk songs | 1028c |
| 73040 | 'Debreczenben jártam én' folk song by Lajos Serly | 1026c |
| 73045 | 'Pling-plong' from the opera *Nöemanczipáczió* | 1027c |
| | **Budapest, 1903 (10″)** | |
| GC73199 | 'Eltörött a kis bögre' from the operetta *Szeneslegény szeneslány* | 962z |
| GC73203 | 'Magasan repül a daru' folksong | 967z |
| GC73210 | 'Csókolj édesem' song | 966z |
| GC73227 | 'Madrigal Simonettitöl' from the operetta *Niniss* | 957z |
| GC74008 | 'Az uszás de édes!' from *Niniss* (w. Kornél Sziklai) | 960z |
| GC74009 | Baba duett from the operetta *Oroszlánvadász* (w. Kornl Sziklai) | 961z |
| GC3482 | 'Butterfly' (in English) | 959z |

There are several missing matrix numbers between 957 and 967 in the 1903 10″ Budapest series. There is no way of knowing whether Mme Palmay recorded any other titles at the time.

## CHARLES WORKMAN

Charles Herbert Workman (1873-1923) made his début in the role of Calynx in *Utopia, (Limited)* on tour, and first appeared at the Savoy as Ben Hashbaz in *The Grand Duke* in 1896. He remained with the D'Oyly Carte Company for thirteen years, and was the principal comedian of the touring company for much of that time. He appeared in that capacity at the Savoy in the 1906-7 season and the 1908-9 season. The following season he became an actor-manager, leased the Savoy, and produced three operas, including *Fallen Fairies* by Gilbert and Edward German, in which he also appeared. During this production, he quarrelled with Gilbert over the casting of Nancy McIntosh.

Gilbert wanted Miss McIntosh to play the Fairy Queen. Workman (or the syndicate which backed him) wanted Elsie Spain. Gilbert prevailed – at least at the beginning – and Nancy McIntosh appeared in the opera's première. At the end of the first week, however, she was replaced by her understudy, Amy Evans. Gilbert was furious. He accused Workman of betraying him, and forbade him to appear on the stage in any of his works again. Gilbert's injunction, however, did not apparently apply to recordings, for in the summer of 1910 Workman recorded many of Gilbert's songs for Odeon.

After the quarrel with Gilbert, Workman appeared in the West End in *The Chocolate Soldier, Nightbirds* [*Fledermaus*], and *The Girl in the Taxi.* He continued his career in Australia in 1914. He had a pleasing and well-trained high baritone voice. He is one of the most musical singers ever to play the comedy roles, as his subsequent career in operetta would suggest.

His recordings were probably hastily made. This is suggested by the fact that he omits a line in 'My Name is John Wellington Wells' and he omits a verse in 'A Private Buffoon'. It is odd that these errors were not corrected for his recordings are excellent.

### Odeon, 1910 (10¾")

| | | |
|---|---|---|
| 0639 | *Iolanthe.* 'The Dream Song' [e.g. 'The Nightmare Song'] | Lx3303 |
| 0639 | *The Mikado.* 'Tit Willow' | Lx3305 |
| 0648 | *The Pirates of Penzance.* 'The Major-General's Song' | Lx3304 |
| 0648 | *H.M.S. Pinafore.* 'When I was a Lad' | Lx3346 |
| 0661 | *Princess Ida.* 'If You Give Me Your Attention' | Lx3301* |
| 0661 | *Trial by Jury.* 'The Judge's Song' | Lx3350 |
| 0676 | *The Sorcerer.* 'My Name is John Wellington Wells' | Lx3348 |
| 0676 | *The Gondoliers.* 'In Enterprise of Martial Kind' | Lx3349 |
| 0685 | *The Yeomen of the Guard.* 'A Private Buffoon' | Lx3302 |
| 0685 | *Patience.* 'Bunthorne's Song' (w. Recit.) | Lx3347 |

10" Odeon by Charles Workman. A song he never sang onstage.

(continued over)

**Charles Workman (cont.)**

[The next four selections are from *The Chocolate Soldier* in which Workman was at the time appearing.]

| 0704 | 'That Would Be Loverly' (w. Evelyn d'Alroy) | Lx3517 |
|---|---|---|
| 0704 | 'The Letter Song' (w. Evelyn d'Alroy) | Lx3518 |
| 0705 | 'The Tale of a Coat' (w. d'Alroy, Amy Augarde, Tom Shale, and Lempriere Pringle) | Lx3531 |
| 0705 | Finale Act II (w. same cast) | Lx3533 |
| 0730 | *Iolanthe.* 'The Law is the True Embodiment' | Lx3592 |
| 0730 | *Iolanthe.* 'When I Went to the Bar' | Lx3593 |
| 0743 | *The Pirates of Penzance.* 'Softly Sighing to the River' | Lx3591 |
| 0743 | *The Yeomen of the Guard.* 'I Have a Song to Sing Oh' (w. Elsie Spain) | |

**Odeon, 1912 (10")**

| 0809 | *The Gondoliers.* 'I Stole the Prince' | LxG88 |
|---|---|---|
| 0809 | *The Yeomen of the Guard.* 'I've Jibe and Joke | LxG91 |
| 0841 | *Utopia, (Limited).* 'Some Seven Men' | LxG86 |
| 0841 | *Princess Ida.* 'Whene'er I Poke Sarcastic Joke' | LxG87 |
| 0851 | *Utopia, (Limited).* 'First You're Born' | LxG89 |
| 0851 | *The Rose of Persia.* 'The Small Street Arab' | LxG90 |

The six records immediately above are with Herman Finck's Orchestra.
All of Workman's Odeons are double-sided discs.

*Two takes of this song were recorded: Lx 3301 and Lx 3301-2. Both were issued.

---

# ISABEL JAY

Isabel Jay (1879-1927) made occasional appearances as Elsie and Gianetta at the Savoy in 1897. She became leading soprano there upon the departure of Ruth Vincent in 1899. She replaced Ellen Beach Yaw in *The Rose of Persia* and then appeared in *The Pirates of Penzance, Patience,* and *Iolanthe.*

Upon leaving the Savoy in 1902 she appeared in several West End musicals including *A Country Girl, The Cingalee, Veronique,* and *The White Chrysanthemum.* She retired from the stage in 1911.

**20 December 1900, Berliner**

| 3214 | 'Poor Wand'ring One' | | 1850a |
|---|---|---|---|

**Black G & T, 7 April 1904**

| GC3523 | *The Cingalee.* 'You and I' | CR | 5137b |
|---|---|---|---|
| unissued | *The Country Girl.* 'Coo' | CR | 5136b |
| unissued | 'Glee Maiden' | | 5138b |

### 21 April 1904

| GC3527 | The Cingalee. 'My Heart's at Your Feet' | | CR | 5227b |
| GC3528 | The Pirates of Penzance. 'Poor Wand'ring One' | | | 5230b |
| GC3530 | The Country Girl. 'Coo' | | CR | 5228b |
| unissued | 'When Jack and I Were Children' | | | 5229b |
| unissued | The Country Girl. 'Coo' | CR | (7") | 6165a |
| unissued | The Cingalee. 'My Heart's at Your Feet' | | CR | 5226b |

### 16 September 1904

| GC3566 | The Cingalee. 'My Heart's at Your Feet' | CR | 5853b |
| unissued | The Cingalee. 'My Heart's at Your Feet' | | 5854b |
| GC3567 | The Pirates of Penzance. 'Poor Wand'ring One' | | 5852b |
| unissued | The Pirates of Penzance. 'Poor Wand'ring One' | | 5851b |

### 14 March 1905

| GC4372 | The Cingalee. 'A Marriage Has Been Arranged' (w. Bradfield) | CR | 1942e |
| GC4372X | The Cingalee. A Marriage Has Been Arranged' (w. Bradfield) | CR | 1941e |
| GC4373 | The Cingalee. 'You and I' (w. Louis Bradfield) | CR | 1943e |
| unissued | The Cingalee. 'My Heart's at Your Feet' (w. Bradfield) | CR | 1939-40e |

### Edison Bell Cylinders, 1906

| 6839 | 'When Jack and I were Children' |
| 6649 | 'While I am Waiting' |
| 6650 | 'Take Estelle and Veronique' |

### Favourite, 1906

| 1-66014 | The Girl Behind the Counter. 'I Want to Marry a Man' | CR | 1931-0 |
| 1-66016 | The White Chrysanthemum. 'The Wandering Breeze' | CR | 1930-0 |
| 1-69003 | The Girl Behind the Counter. 'Won't You Buy' (w. E. Gordon Cleather) | CR | 1926-0 |
| 1-66012 | Veronique. 'While I am Waiting' | | 1927-0 |
| 1-66013 | 'Goodbye' (Tosti) | | 1929-0 |

## BLANCHE GASTON MURRAY

Blanche Gaston Murray was the daughter of Gaston Murray, a well-known 'leading man' of the nineteenth century, who appeared in *Dr. Dulcamera*, Gilbert's first professional production, at the St James's Theatre in 1867.

Miss Murray played Tessa at the Savoy in the 1898 revival of *The Gondoliers*, and Angela in *Patience* in 1900. She was the leading soubrette in the tours of 1899 and 1900, appearing as Iolanthe, Pitti-Sing, and others. Her sister was married to Courtice Pounds.

**28 February 1905**

| | | |
|---|---|---|
| GC4371 | *Veronique.* 'Swing Song' (w. Arthur Grover) | 1854e |
| unissued | *Veronique.* 'We'll try and be Precise' (w. Arthur Grover) | 1899-1900e |

## LOUIE POUNDS

Louie Pounds was the youngest sister of Courtice Pounds. She made her début in George Edwardes' production of *A Gaiety Girl.* She then appeared in *An Artist's Model* in which she toured America. She was seldom out of work in a stage career that lasted from 1890 to 1929.

In 1899 she joined the D'Oyly Carte Company and appeared in *The Rose of Persia, The Emerald Isle, Merrie England,* and *A Princess of Kensington.* She played the title role in the 1901 revival of *Iolanthe.* Thereafter she had a successful career in West End musicals, appearing in *The Earl and the Girl, The White Chrysanthemum, The Belle of Mayfair,* and the revival of *Dorothy.* She toured in *The Merry Widow,* and played the title role in *The Golden Girl* by Basil Hood. She is known to have made only one recording.

**Pathé Cylinder, 1905**

| | | |
|---|---|---|
| 41050 | *The Earl and the Girl.* 'Sammy' | |
| | (w. Adelphi Theatre Chorus) | CR |

## ROBERT EVETT

Robert Evett (1874-1949) made his début in 1893 in a D'Oyly Carte touring Company. Soon he became the principal tenor on tour. He first appeared at the Savoy in 1898 and remained there as leading tenor until 1903, appearing in *The Gondoliers, The Sorcerer, The Rose of Persia, The Emerald Isle, Iolanthe, Merrie England* and *A Princess of Kensington.*

In the next few years he starred in West End productions of *The Earl and the Girl, The Little Michus, The Merry Widow,* and *A Waltz Dream.* On the death of George Edwardes he became a manager of Daly's Theatre and later of the Gaiety. He had the distinction of giving Martyn Green his first job in the theatre.

At the end of his life he was cheered enormously when his wife found in a London second-hand shop some of the recordings which he had made forty years earlier.

(continued over)

**Robert Evett (cont.)**

**Odeon, 1906 (10¾")**

| | | | |
|---|---|---|---|
| 44055* | *The Little Michus.* | | |
| | 'It's No Use Crying for the Moon' | CR | Lx1194 |
| 44168 | *A Princess of Kensington.* 'A Sprig of Rosemary' | CR | Lx1358 |
| 44189 | *Merrie England.* 'The English Rose' | CR | Lx1350 |
| 44191 | *Cigarette.* 'Oh How I Love Thee' | | Lx1356 |
| 44165 | 'Thou Art My Rose' | | Lx1352 |
| 44192 | *Talk of the Town.* 'For You' | CR | Lx1359 |
| | 608   'Bring Back the Sunshine'** | | |
| | 608   'Mother o'Mine' | | |

**Odeon, 1907-8 (10¾")**

| | | | |
|---|---|---|---|
| 44603 | A307 *The Yeomen of the Guard.* 'Is Life a Boon?' | | Lx1837 |
| 44604 | A307 *The Yeomen of the Guard.* | | |
| | 'Free From His Fetters Grim' *** | | Lx1838 |
| 44632 | 0240 *The Geisha.* 'Star of my Soul' | | Lx1839 |
| 66079 | 0240 *The Merry Widow.* 'Home' | CR | Lx2353-2 |
| 66080 | 0322 *The Merry Widow.* 'A Dutiful Wife' Pt. 1 | | |
| | (w. Elizabeth Firth) | CR | Lx2354-2 |
| 66081 | 0322 *The Merry Widow.* 'A Dutiful Wife' Pt. 2 | | |
| | (w. Elizabeth Firth) | CR | Lx2355 |
| 66082 | 0321 *The Merry Widow.* | | |
| | 'Love in my Heart Awaking' Pt. 1 | | |
| | (w. Elizabeth Firth) | CR | Lx2356-2 |
| 66083 | 0321 *The Merry Widow.* | | |
| | 'Love in my Heart Awaking' Pt. 2 | | |
| | (w. Elizabeth Firth) | CR | Lx2357-2 |
| 66315 | 0413 *A Waltz Dream.* 'The Dream Waltz' | CR | Lx2643-2 |
| 66289 | 0413 *A Waltz Dream.* 'My Dear Little Maiden' | CR | Lx2644 |

*The English Odeon 44000 and 66000 numbers were 'side' numbers. The original three digit catalogue numbers were in time replaced by a new three digit number preceded by the letter A. This was replaced by a four digit catalogue number beginning with 0. All of Robert Evett's Odeon records were issued in double-sided form.
** Until a copy of this record turns up, the side and matrix numbers will remain unknown.
***Two takes of this song were recorded: Lx1818 and Lx1818-2. Both were issued.

# THE SAVOY OPERA CHORUS, 1900

The first recording session of the D'Oyly Carte Opera Company took place in December of 1900! From all accounts it appears to have been a rather casual affair. Walter Passmore had visited the Gramophone

Company studios on 19 December and made two 7" records. On 20 December a few (unidentified) members of the Company, led by Isabel Jay, made three more. The first was 'Poor Wand'ring One' (or most of it anyway) for which Miss Jay received credit on the label. Two sides from *Patience* were then recorded. The etched labels, however, only say 'Chorus of Maidens' and 'Soldiers of Our Queen', information which is not wholly accurate.

The first excerpt from *Patience* includes the chorus 'The Soliders of our Queen' and almost all of the solo 'A Heavy Dragoon'. The second includes the last two numbers in the printed score, 'I'm a Waterloo House Young Man' and the Finale, sung twice. These records were issued as by the "Savoy Opera Chorus", a Gramophone Company designation.

The entire Savoy Chorus of course did not participate in these recordings. There was only one recording horn into which all the performers had to sing. The larger the number of voices to be recorded, the more distant the singers would have had to be from the horn, and the weaker the soloists would sound – and the more difficult they would be to identify.

The principals appearing in *Patience* in December of 1900 included:

| | |
|---|---|
| Grosvenor | Henry Lytton |
| Bunthorne | Walter Passmore |
| Duke of Dunstable | Robert Evett |
| Colonel Calverly | Charles Childerstone *or* Jones Hewson |
| Patience | Isabel Jay |
| Lady Ella | Agnes Fraser |

Unfortunately the soloists are not identified on the records, and the Gramophone Company's recording sheets for the year 1900 have long since disappeared, making positive identification of these singers virtually impossible.

The singers were accompanied by a studio "orchestra" – which is to say a small number of wind instruments.


### 20 December 1900 (7")

| | | |
|---|---|---|
| 3214 | *The Pirates of Penzance.* 'Poor Wand'ring One' | |
| | (Isabel Jay, soloist) | 1850a |
| 4525 | *Patience.* 'A Heavy Dragoon' | |
| | [Labelled: 'Soliders of Our Queen'] | 1854a |
| 4526 | *Patience.* Finale, Act II | |
| | [Labelled: 'Chorus of Maidens'] | 1855xD(a) |

## THE SAVOY THEATRE IN THE NINETEENTH CENTURY

The Savoy Company in the nineteenth century was a young company. The number of sopranos who appeared there in leading roles before they were twenty-one (Isabel Jay, Decima Moore, Ruth Vincent, for example) was extraordinary. The number of comedians who began playing leading roles while still in their twenties (Walter Passmore, Charles Workman, Henry Lytton) was unusual as well.

Sullivan, however, before his days at the Savoy, had conducted some of the leading orchestras in Great Britain, as well as many of the country's leading concert artists. Gilbert was well established in the London theatre, and had worked with a large number of important performers. Both men agreed at the beginning of their collaboration, that their new company would have no stars.*

Fortunately, earlier in his career, Sullivan had served as the first Principal of the Royal College of Music. The Savoy Theatre was often used by the Royal College for student productions. Sullivan was fond of visiting the great singing teacher, Mathilde Marchesi at her school in Paris, and both the École Marchesi and the Royal College of Music from time to time provided the Savoy with a few excellent young singers who, in Gilbert's words, would have "nothing to unlearn."

That Gilbert and Sullivan were good judges of talent is clear from the large number of performers who went on to successful careers after they left the Savoy. Robert Evett and Charles Workman found constant employment in operetta. Rutland Barrington and Walter Passmore had long careers in musical comedy. George Grossmith returned successfully to the tradition of the drawing-room entertainer. A few artists, like John Coates and Ruth Vincent, became more known for their careers in classical music. Luckily enough of these artists made records in the early days of the gramophone to provide us with some idea of what a performance at the Savoy in the nineteenth century might have been like.

It is clear that the quality of singing at the Savoy was indeed high. The performing style was classical under Sullivan's direction and the link to the traditions of French and Italian opera, at which Sullivan was poking fun, was much clearer at the turn of the century. Tempos were expectably faster and more secure. The recordings of 'personality' tenors, such as Scott Russell and Courtice Pounds make it clear why Gilbert preferred to work with singers who could act.

Listening to the comedians who recorded, it becomes clear that musicianship was not always the most important consideration in the comedy parts, although theatricality certainly was. The level of energy in the recordings of the patter songs is generally astonishing, and the rapid changes of inflection, often dazzling. What is more, there is a likableness in the voices of Workman and Lytton which evokes a smile from the listener no matter what song is being sung. And the diction is – predictably – immaculate.

Rutland Barrington, in his one and only recording, achieves an extraordinary degree of urbanity with decidedly little effort. It only makes us wish that he had recorded more. Nonetheless, the cylinder is enough to establish a striking similarity between his style and that of Leo Sheffield, his successor. Rutland Barrington's two-minute cylinder provides the link between W.S. Gilbert and the large recorded legacy of Leo Sheffield.

It would appear from these early recordings, that the comedy was broader under Gilbert's direction and the music more classical under Sullivan's. The extremes of farce and pathos in a nineteenth century production would have certainly been greater than in a recent performance, and the consequent changes in dynamics from one moment to the next, would probably have astonished a modern audience. Of course the size of the theatre and the performing company would have intensified this effect.

It is well to remember that the Savoy operas were written for a theatre that seated under 1000 people. As originally designed, the Savoy had three balconies, and the distance from the farthest seat to any point on the stage was never very great. Consequently, when Rutland Barrington made a funny face, it could be seen from the rear of the gallery. What is more, the operas were presented in London with a chorus of forty and an orchestra of thirty. The effect of such large forces in a house so small could only have been breathtaking. With all of these elements working for the operas in their day, it is little wonder that after hundred years they remain the most popular English stage works of their century. And yet when, as is so often the case in recent productions, we see a Gilbert and Sullivan opera given with half the forces which Gilbert and Sullivan themselves employed, and presented in a hall two or three times larger, we have to assume that we are receiving only a fraction of the effect which Sullivan and Gilbert themselves achieved. The records made by the singers they trained suggest that this is true.

*One rare exception to this policy, the hiring of Lillian Russell for the lead in *Princess Ida*, resulted only in trouble [p70].

During the 1890s Sullivan wrote *Ivanhoe, Haddon Hall, The Chieftain, The Beauty Stone,* and *The Rose of Persia,* all independently of Gilbert. Similarly, Gilbert wrote *Haste to the Wedding, The Mountebanks,* and *His Excellency* independently of Sullivan. Various singers who appeared in one or more of these productions under the direction of Gilbert or Sullivan also made recordings.

The following six singers appeared in Sullivan operas.

# BEN DAVIES

Ben Davies (1858-1943) sang with the Carl Rosa Company from 1881 to 1885, and then appeared in the premières of *Dorothy* and *Doris*, both with music by Alfred Cellier, one of the first conductors of the D'Oyly Carte Company.* In 1890 Sullivan chose Ben Davies to be the leading tenor of the Royal English Opera, where he sang the title role in *Ivanhoe*.

Davies sang for Queen Victoria at Windsor in 1892 and at the Chicago World's Fair in 1893. Thereafter he devoted himself primarily to concert performances. He appeared in the première of the song-cycle *In a Persian Garden* with Emma Albani and David Bispham. Sullivan was obviously fond of Ben Davies, for he invited him to sing at the Leeds Festival in 1892, 1895 and 1898.

Davies had a long recording career, beginning with Pathé at the turn of the century, and continuing with the Gramophone Company into the electric era. Only his Sullivan records are listed here.

|  | **G & T, 11 November 1902** |  |
|---|---|---|
| GC2-2782 | 'The Sailor's Grave' | 2727b |
| unissued | 'The Sailor's Grave' | 2726b |
|  | **Pathé, 1903-4** |  |
| 60010 | *The Gondoliers*. 'Take a Pair of Sparkling Eyes' |  |
| 60020 | 'The Sailor's Grave' |  |
|  | **Pathé, 1905-6** |  |
| 60050 | *The Gondoliers*. 'Take a Pair of Sparkling Eyes' |  |
|  | **Pathé, 1906-7** |  |
| 77168 | *The Martyr of Antioch*. 'Come Margarita, Come' |  |

---

*Ben Davies recorded only one song from his stage career, and it was by Cellier, not Sullivan:

|  | **G & T, 1903** |  |  |
|---|---|---|---|
| 2-2781 | *Doris*. 'So Fare Thee Well' | CR | 2725-2W |
|  | **Pathé, 1903** |  |  |
| 60007 | *Doris*. 'So Fare Thee Well' | CR |  |

## JOSEPH O'MARA

Joseph O'Mara (1866-1927) at the age of twenty-four, alternated with Ben Davies in the role of *Ivanhoe* at the Royal English Opera, and then went on to a successful career in opera and light opera. He sang the lead in *Cavalleria Rusticana* and *Faust* with Esther Palliser at Covent Garden in 1893, and in the next two seasons appeared at Drury Lane in *Maritana*, *The Lily of Killarney* and *Philemon et Baucis* (the latter with David Bispham and Charles Manners). The next season he appeared in *Fra Diavolo* at Covent Garden with de Lucia, and in 1896 sang in the famous production of *Shamus O'Brien* C.V. Stanford. The stage manager of that production was Richard Temple.

|  | **December 1901** |  |  |
|---|---|---|---|
| GC2-2567 | *Shamus O'Brien.* 'Ochone! When I used to be Young' | | |
|  | (Stanford) | CR | 1229b |
| 2-2062 | 'Friend and Lover' (Ronald) | (7") | 4144a |
| 2-2061 | 'An April Birthday' (Ronald) | (7") | 4143a |
|  | **May 1911** | | |
| unissued | 'Eleanore' (Coleridge-Taylor) | (12") | 5040f |

---

## FLORENCE ST. JOHN

Florence St. John (1854-1912) first sang professionally at the age of fourteen, the age at which she was first married. At twenty-one she first appeared in London, making a hit with Sullivan's song 'Once Again' in a Variety bill at the Oxford Theatre.

By the 1890s she had become a major West End star in light opera and musical comedy. She appeared at the Savoy in *Mirette*, *The Grand Duchess of Gerolstein*, and *The Chieftain.* In 1900 she appeared in the famous production of *Florodora*, the source her only known recording.

|  | **3 October 1900** (7") | |
|---|---|---|
| 3200 | *Florodora.* 'He Loves Me; He Loves Me Not' | |
|  | (Piano acc. Leslie Stuart) | 1444a |

## BARTON McGUCKIN

Barton McGuckin (1853-1913) first sang for Sullivan in the Bach B Minor Mass at the Leeds Festival of 1886. In 1891 he sang the title role in *Ivanhoe* when it was revived at the Royal English Opera. He was the leading tenor with the Carl Rosa Opera Company for several seasons, where his roles included Tannhäuser, Lohengrin, and Don José in *Carmen*. He was also a popular festival and concert singer.

His records, unfortunately, were made late in his career. They are extremely rare, and, collectors agree, extremely disappointing. The fact that they were issued on the lower priced Zonophone label suggests that the Gramophone Company found them disappointing too. By 1899 McGuckin had already begun producing opera, and his career as a singer had more or less ended. The records, however, do suggest that he was an exciting singer in his day.

These three tenors whom Sullivan chose for *Ivanhoe* (as well as Edward Lloyd who sang the tenor parts in his oratorios) all had heroic voices and sang with a daring 'uncovered' foreward placement. It was courageous singing, and apparently not nearly so uncommon in the nineteenth century as it has become today.

**Green Zonophone, 25 February 1905**

| | | |
|---|---|---|
| X42279 | 'Avenging and Bright' (Moore) | 1849e |
| X42280 | 'Savourneen Delish' (Dufferin) | 1848e |
| unissued | 'Lanagan's Log' (Lohr) | 1850e |

## DAVID BISPHAM

David Bispham (1857-1921) was an American baritone who studied with Lamperti in Milan. In the spring of 1891 when Bispham was accepting concert engagements in London, Richard D'Oyly Carte offered him the role of Cedric in *Ivanhoe* replacing Frangcon Davies who had begun drinking more than the management of the Royal English Opera would have liked. Bispham, however, felt uncomfortable at the thought of taking a role away from a fellow singer under such circumstances, and he declined. Nevertheless, he was hired that autumn, and made his stage début as the Duke in *La Basoche*, an operetta which alternated briefly with *Ivanhoe*.

After leaving the Royal English Opera, he continued his studies and became a leading Wagnerian baritone and appeared with great success in America and in Europe. After 1903 he devoted himself to a highly successful career as a concert and oratorio singer. He made a large number of recordings for Columbia, including the following two recollections of his Royal English Opera days.

**Columbia, U.S.A. c. 1909**

| A5099 | *Ivanhoe*. 'Ho Jolly Jenkin' | 30218 |
| A5137 | *Ivanhoe*. 'Woo Thou Thy Snowflake' | 30287 |

## ELLEN BEACH YAW

Ellen Beach Yaw (1869-1947) was an American pupil of Mathilde Marchesi. Miss Yaw had a coloratura voice with an extended upper register. At Sullivan's urging she was cast as the Sultana in *The Rose of Persia* in 1899. Sullivan wrote a special cadenza, not printed in the score, for her in the song, "Neath My Lattice'.

Miss Yaw, however, did not make a good impression at the opening night of the opera and Mrs. D'Oyly Carte wanted to fire her. Sullivan was less anxious to do so, and wrote in his diary during the second week of performances, "Having listened all the week through the telephone to the Opera, I find Miss Yaw improving rapidly every night.* Last night she sang the song really superbly – brilliant..." Nevertheless, Mrs. D'Oyly Carte dismissed her the next day over Sullivan's objection, and Miss Yaw was understandably upset. In fact, the 1915 edition of *Who's Who in Music* claimed that she "was heard for the first time in London at the Queen's Hall under Sir Henry Wood in 1902"!

Her experience at the Savoy may have ruined her taste for opera. She sang one single performance of *Lucia di Lammermoor* at the Metropolitan in New York, 21 March 1908, with Bonci. Thereafter, she confined herself to concert tours in the United States and Canada.

Mme Yaw made eight 7" records in March of 1899, a few months before her Savoy appearance, which preserve the quality of her voice at the time that Sullivan heard it and was impressed by it. Her later records, made after several years had separated her from her Marchesi training, are far less impressive.

---

*In the late eighties, at Gilbert's suggestion, Sullivan had a telephone installed in his flat at Queens Mansions. From there he could communicate with the Savoy Theatre where there was a telephone in the box office as well as backstage. Through the latter it was possible to hear the performance onstage.

### 11 March 1899

| | | |
|---|---|---|
| E3095 | *Flute Enchantée.* 'Air de la reine de la nuit' | 1576 |
| E3096 | 'O dolce contento' | 1577 |
| E3096X | 'O dolce contento' | 1570 |
| E3097 | *Manon Lescaut.* 'Laughing Song' (Auber) | 1574 |

### 13 March 1899

| | | |
|---|---|---|
| E3101 | 'Tarentelle' | |
| E3102 | 'Swiss Echo Song' | |
| E3104 | 'Air de la vision' (Fransella, flute) | 1606 |

### 18 March 1899

| | | |
|---|---|---|
| E3105 | Cadenza from *Étoile du Nord* (Meyerbeer) (Fransella, flute) | 1657 |
| E3106 | *Les Noces de Jeanette.* 'Chanson du Rossignol' (Massé) | 1660 |

All of the above are 7" records belonging to the early "unlettered" matrix series.

The prefix letter 'E' indicates merely that these records were recorded in England, although sung in French or Italian.

## SINGERS AT LEEDS

Outside of the Savoy, Arthur Sullivan enjoyed the reputation of one of England's leading classical musicians. As such, his most important appointment was that of Conductor and General Music Director of the Leeds Triennial Music Festival, a position which he held from 1877 to 1898. The famous Leeds Festival Choir, composed of three hundred Welsh, Lancashire and Yorkshire voices, was frequently called the finest chorus in the world. At the Leeds Music Festival, the featured work was always the oratorio.

During the reign of Queen Victoria the oratorio achieved unparalled popularity. Sullivan composed four oratorios, two of which he presented at Leeds. In the eighties England's leading concert singers (known in fact as the 'Oratorio Quartet') were Emma Albani, Janet Patey, Edward Lloyd and Charles Santley. They were all friends of Sullivan, and frequent guest artists at Leeds. It was of course the Oratorio Quartet which appeared there in the premières of Sullivan's oratorios, *The Martyr of Antioch* (1880) and *The Golden Legend* (1886).

*The Martyr of Antioch* faded quickly into oblivion, but *The Golden Legend* achieved a tremendous popularity which, for a few years in the nineties rivalled that of *The Messiah.* Sullivan conducted *The Golden Legend* many times with the original performers, including a Command Performance for Queen Victoria at the Albert Hall in May 1888. Of the original Oratorio Quartet, all but Janet Patey, who died in 1894, eventually made records.

The standard of singing at the Leeds Festival under Sullivan was as high as could be found in Britain, and it was no accident that Sullivan never asked anyone who had first sung for him at the Savoy Theatre to appear at Leeds. He did, however, invite four members of the cast of *Ivanhoe* to sing there: Esther Palliser, Ben Davies, Barton McGuckin and David Bispham. The records which they made are listed earlier. Other artists who appeared with Sullivan at Leeds and later made recordings included Clara Butt, Ada Crossley, Andrew Black, and William Green. And it should perhaps be mentioned that the famous Leeds Festival Choir, which Sullivan had conducted from 1877 to 1898, made three records in 1907.

*Only recordings of Sullivan's music*
*is listed by the singers who follow.*

# CLARA BUTT

Clara Butt (1873-1936) studied at the Royal College of Music, of which Sullivan had been the first Principal. She made her stage début in 1892 at the age of nineteen in the famous Royal College production of *Orfeo* (directed by Richard Temple). She made her concert début the same season in *The Golden Legend* at the Albert Hall. She is one of the few artists to sing before an audience with Arthur Sullivan as her accompanist. Sullivan played for her at one of the soirées in the home of Mrs. Ronalds, a well-known American hostess. She sang a few more performances of *The Golden Legend* in London in the early nineties before going to Paris to study.

In 1898 Sullivan contracted her to sing in *Elijah* which was the opening work of the Leeds Festival that year. The following entry appears in his Diary for 8 October:

> *Leeds.* 1st day of Festival.
> God Save the Queen and Elijah. Clara Butt was to sing the whole contralto part, but, not having thought it necessary to ascertain what time it began, was not there. I saw Ada Crossley sitting below me – beckoned to her and got her up to sing the part. At the end of the 1st part I found Clara Butt in my room crying her heart out at her folly. I didn't say much to her but I told her she could sing the 2nd part.*

Clara Butt made a large number of recordings for the Gramophone Company beginning in 1910, and later for Columbia. Only her Sullivan recordings are listed here, with one addition. In 1900, ten years before her recording career began in earnest, she made a single 7″ record with her husband, the baritone Kennerley Rumford. This provides us with a unique example of her voice at the time that Sullivan heard and admired it. It is a far lighter sound than is heard on her later records.

*From the *Diaries of Arthur Sullivan* [MS], Beinecke Library, Yale University. Clara Butt tells the story rather differently in her biography (p. 244)! See bibliography.

| | **Berliner, 26 January 1899** (7″) | |
|---|---|---|
| 4054 | 'Night Hymn at Sea' (Goring Thomas) | |
| | (w. Kennerley Rumford) | 1040 |

| | **HMV** (12″) | |
|---|---|---|
| 03151 | 'The Lost Chord' [c. 1909] | 3482f |
| 03224 | 'Will He Come' (w. piano and organ) [October 1910] | 4559f |
| 03399 | *The Light of the World.* 'God Shall Wipe Away All Tears' | Ho667c |

(continued over)

**Clara Butt (cont.)**

| | | **Columbia, before 1916** (12″) | |
|---|---|---|---|
| 7100 | 7301 | 'The Lost Chord' (w. piano and organ) | 6544 |
| | 7301* | 'The Lost Chord' (w. orchestra) [1924] | AX375 |
| 7104 | 7302 | *The Light of the World.* | 6555 |
| | | 'God Shall Wipe Away All Tears' | |

| | | **Columbia, before 1916** (12″) | |
|---|---|---|---|
| | X326 | 'The Willow Song' (Shakespeare) | A2205 |

| | **Columbia, 1928** (12″) | |
|---|---|---|
| 7374(a) | *The Light of the World.* | |
| | 'God Shall Wipe Away All Tears' | WAX3052 |
| 7374(b)* | *The Light of the World.* | |
| | 'God Shall Wipe Away All Tears' | WAX3052 |
| 7375 | 'The Lost Chord' | WAX3054 |

[The numbers in the left column are of the single-sided issues. The numbers in the inner column are of the double-sided issues.]

*Columbia was notorious for issuing later recordings of the same title under the same record number, and often under the same matrix number.

# EDWARD LLOYD

Edward Lloyd (1845-1927) was the outstanding Festival tenor of his day. His first important success was in Bach's *Saint Matthew Passion* at the Gloucester Festival of 1871. For most of his professional career (which lasted almost thirty years) he was without rival on the concert stage. Sullivan invited him to perform at Leeds repeatedly. In addition to singing in the premières of two Sullivan oratorios, he appeared in the first performances of Gounod's *The Redemption*, Dvorak's *Saint Ludmilla*, and *Caractacus* and *The Dream of Gerontius* by Elgar. He never appeared in opera, and when he retired in 1900, there was no tenor his equal to follow him in the concert hall.

Edward Lloyd did not begin recording until 1903, but over the next three years he made about thirty-five records for the Gramophone Company. Only one was of Sullivan's music.

**Black G & T, 1907**

| | | | |
|---|---|---|---|
| GC3-2855 | *The Martyr of Antioch.* 'Come Margarita, Come' | CR | 10080b |

## ADA CROSSLEY

Ada Crossley (1874-1929) was born in Australia and came to Europe to study with Santley and Marchesi. She made her début in London in 1895. In 1899 she sang in the Handel Oratorio *Alexander's Feast* for Sullivan at the Leeds Festival where she also deputized for the absent Clara Butt. Ada Crossley appeared regularly at English Festivals until 1913 where she frequently sang in *The Apostles, Elijah*, and the Bach B Minor Mass.

She recorded four titles for Victor and six more for Pathé in 1904. She is one of the few Marchesi contraltos on record. Ada Crossley was dropped from the most recent edition of *Grove's Dictionary.*

| | **Pathé, 1904** | |
|---|---|---|
| 50293 | 'The Lost Chord' (w. organ and piano) | 20453 |
| 50293 | 'The Lost Chord' (w. orchestra) | 29798 |


## CHARLES SANTLEY

Charles Santley (1834-1922) made his début in Handel's oratorio, *The Creation* in 1857. Shortly thereafter he became Britain's leading Festival baritone, a position in which he was virtually unchallenged for over forty years. He sang repeatedly at the Leeds Festival, the Norwich Festival, the Birmingham Festival, and the Three Choirs Festival. He appeared at every Handel Festival at the Crystal Palace from 1862 to 1904. He had an equally distinguished career in opera both in England and on the Continent. Gounod wrote the music to 'Even Bravest Heart' ('*Avant de quitter des leiux*') specially for him prior to the English première of *Faust.*

Santley was also a well-loved singer of ballads. He introduced 'Thou Art Passing Hence' to the public in 1875 and sang it at the Leeds Festival two years later. Years after Sullivan's death, Santley was still receiving royalties from the sale of the music to this song.

Charles Santley was the first singer to be knighted. He made five records for the Gramophone Company in 1903 when he was seventy. He made a few more records for Columbia at the end of the decade. He is one of very few students of Manuel Garcia on record.

| | **G & T Red (later Black) Label, 1903** | |
|---|---|---|
| 02015 | 'Thou'rt Passing Hence, My Brother' | WCG188R |

# ANDREW BLACK

Andrew Black (1859-1920) made his début at the Crystal Palace in 1887, but his career did not become firmly established until he sang in Dvorak's cantata, *The Spectre's Bride*, at the Leeds Festival of 1892. Thereafter he was a popular Festival and concert singer, famous for his performance of *Elijah* (which he sang at Leeds in 1895). He was the most popular singer of the oratorio after Santley. He created the role of Caractacus in Elgar's cantata of the same name (Leeds Festival, 1898) and he was the first Judas in *The Apostles* (Birmingham Festival, 1903). He was frequently the soloist when Sullivan's incidental music to *Henry VIII* was presented in concert. Sullivan admired his performance of 'King Henry's Song'.

Andrew Black recorded about forty sides for the Gramophone Company between 1901 and 1906, and a few sides for Columbia.

### Black G & T, April 1902

| | | |
|---|---|---|
| GC2-2651 | *The Sorcerer.* 'The Curate's Song' | 1905b |
| GC2-2652 | 'Thou'rt Passing Hence, My Brother' | 1906b |

### 11 August 1904

| | | |
|---|---|---|
| GC3-2107 | *Henry VIII.* 'King Henry's Song' | |
| | ('Youth Must Needs Have Dalliance', words by Henry VIII) | 5533b |
| GC3-2115 | *Ivanhoe.* 'Woo Thou Thy Snowflake' | 5530b |

### 1906

| | | |
|---|---|---|
| GC3-2327 | *The Sorcerer.* 'The Curate's Song' | 2487e |

# WILLIAM GREEN

William Green (1868-1920) was (along with Ben Davies and John Coates) one of the more promising of the new generation of concert tenors active when Edward Lloyd retired in 1900. He sang in Bach's B Minor Mass, and Beethoven's Ninth Symphony for Sullivan at Leeds in 1898. He knew Gilbert. He was the father of Martyn Green. He recorded seven titles in 1901 and 1902, and about as many again two years later. The early records are very rare, and the later records unissued, probably because Edward Lloyd began recording in 1903.

### Black G & T

| | | |
|---|---|---|
| GC2-2648 | 'The Sailor's Grave' [1902] | 1499b |
| unissued | 'Once Again' [7 January 1904] | 4850b |
| unissued | 'The Sailor's Grave' [February 1904] | 5105b |

## EMMA ALBANI

Marie Louise Cécelie Emma Lajeunesse (1847-1930) was born near Montreal of French Canadian parents. At the age of fourteen she moved to Albany, New York (hence her stage name) where she sang solos in the church choir. The Bishop there encouraged her to go to Europe to study. She became a pupil of Lamperti in Italy. She made her début in Messina in 1870, and at Covent Garden in La Sonnambula in 1872.

In 1878 she married Ernest Gye, the lessee of Covent Garden, and sang there every season but one from 1880 to 1896. Her repertory included everything from Lucia to Isolde (which she sang with Jean de Reszke). Beginning in 1872, and for more than thirty years, she sang at one or more of the autumn music festivals in England. There, with Santley, Lloyd and Mme Patey, she appeared in the premières of many important oratorios. She was a favourite singer of Queen Victoria.

Emma Albani was a close friend of Sullivan's and sang for him many times at Leeds. In 1877 Sullivan cabled her from Germany in desperation. He had just conducted a disastrous performance of The Golden Legend at the Berlin Opera for the Kaiser's birthday. The performance had been completely ruined by the presence of a totally unsuitable German soprano. Sullivan had managed to schedule a second performance of the oratorio at the Opera House, and had even persuaded the German Royal Family (which included Princess Victoria, the eldest daughter of Queen Victoria) to hear the work again if Madame Albani, for whom the soprano part had been written, would agree to come to Berlin to sing it! She did, and when the work was presented a second time, the German audience and press were amazed at how wonderful the oratorio, which they had so disliked the week before, actually was. Emma Albani's presence had somehow galvanized the entire performance.

Mme. Albani recorded several titles for the Gramophone Company and Pathé in 1903 and 1904. She recorded no music of Sullivan. It is difficult to appreciate now, when Sullivan's reputation rests exclusively upon his work at the Savoy, how important a reputation he had as a serious musician in his lifetime. But the Victorian music festivals were major events in their day; the oratorio was the highest form of musical art; and Charles Santley, Emma Albani and Edward Lloyd were among the most popular singers in Britain. And if, in the last decade of the nineteenth century, the three most frequently performed oratorios were Elijah, The Messiah, and The Golden Legend, it would be difficult to regard Sullivan's

(continued over)

**Emma Albani (cont.)**

contribution to the serious musical life of England as minor.

Even as late as the First World War the three most recorded oratorios continued to be *Elijah*, *The Messiah*, and *The Golden Legend*. Between 1908 and 1913 no less than seven selections from *The Golden Legend* were recorded by the Gramophone Company (unfortunately not by any singers who had worked with Sullivan).*

The Leeds Music Festival ended in 1950. It reached its highest popularity in the late 1880s and 90s under Sullivan's direction. Nineteenth century singing was in many ways different from that of the present day, and it is fortunate that at least a small sample of its traditions have been preserved by the gramophone.

The best known recording from *The Golden Legend* is 'The Night is Calm' sung by the Wagnerian soprano Florence Austrel in 1926. D1506 (electric) mat CR2167, John Barbirolli, cond.

*As a final footnote to this section two further artists are worthy of note. W.M. Malsch, the oboist who played the oboe d'amore for Sullivan's presentation of the Bach B Minor Mass (with original instruments) at Leeds, recorded for Grammavox. (He may also have been 'Master Malsch', co-soloist with Sullivan at the Chapel Royal.)

Georg Henschel, who sang in *The Golden Legend* in London in the nineties with Sullivan conducting, recorded for the Gramophone Company and Columbia. He was at various times the teacher of Nancy McIntosh and the first Conductor of the Boston Symphony.

---

# GILBERT WITHOUT SULLIVAN

Gilbert was always far more satisfied than Sullivan with their work at the Savoy. Although Gilbert had written several verse plays in the 1870s, and often complained bitterly that they had not been better received, he did not attempt to follow a higher muse after his reputation with Sullivan was firmly established.

In the nineties, therefore, during the famous 'Carpet Quarrel' and its aftermath, Gilbert wrote three operas in more or less the Savoy tradition: *The Mountebanks* with Alfred Cellier (1892), *His Excellency* with Osmond Carr (1894), and *Haste to the Wedding*, an adaptation of *The Italian Straw Hat* with music by George Grossmith (1892)! Some of the artists who appeared in these productions also made records.

W. S. Gilbert.

## LIONEL BROUGH

Lionel Brough (1836-1909) was the uncle of Fanny Brough. His career on the stage lasted over fifty years, during which time he played every kind of part from variety and burlesque (with Toole) to Shakespeare (with Tree). He made his début in 1854 and for thirteen years played mainly in the provinces. After 1867 he appeared in innumerable plays in the West End, his most famous interpretations being Tony Lumpkin in *She Stoops to Conquer* and Bob Acres in *The Rivals*. He appeared in Gilbert's burlesque, *La Vivandière* in 1868, and in the nineties appeared in two Gilbert operas, *Haste to the Wedding* and *The Mountebanks*.

His recordings are all of rather dry anecdotes.

|  | **Edison Bell Cylinders, 1906** |  |
|---|---|---|
| 6934 | 'A Lancashire Story' | |
| 6935 | 'A Sea Story' | |
|  | **Black G & T, 22 September 1906** | |
| GC1323 | 'The Story of Charlie Bacus and Tony Pastor' | 9039b |
| GC1234 | 'Triplets/Dogs in Church' | 9038b |
| GC1328 | 'The Pigeon Story' | 9040b |
|  | **2 November 1906** | |
| GC1362 | 'Calves' Head' | 4796h |
| GC1366 | 'Calves' Head' | 4796½h |
| GC1365 | 'First Sunday After Ascot/Sampling Beer/Cut 'isself Shavin'' | 4795h |
| GC1367 | 'Limberger Cheese' | 4797h |
|  | **1908** | |
| GC1403 | 'A Curate Story' | 8669e |
| GC1404 | 'A Christian Science Story' | 8670e |

## ARTHUR PLAYFAIR

Arthur Playfair (1869-1918), a cousin of Nigel Playfair, was born in India. He made his London début in 1887 and the following year toured with Gilbert's old associates, the Kendals. He appeared in *The Mountebanks* in 1892. He subsequently appeared in many West End successes and in 1904 toured the United States with Charles Hawtrey in *The Man from Blankley's*. Returning to England, he made successful appearances on the Music Halls, and in more London productions including *Bric-à-Brac*, *Vanity Fair*, and *The Passing Show of 1915*.

**Gramophone Company, March 1915**

| | | | |
|---|---|---|---|
| 4-2526 | *The Passing Show of 1915.* 'J.J. Juggernaut' | CR B482 | Ho1329ae |
| 04124 | *The Passing Show of 1915.* | | |

'When the Clock Strikes Thirteen'
(w. Basil Hallam, Nelson Keyes, Douglas Phillips)

|  |  | CR C564 | Ho733af |
|---|---|---|---|

**October 1915**

| 04136 | *Bric-à-Brac.* 'The Optimist and the Pessimist' | | |
|---|---|---|---|
| | (w. Nelson Keys) | CR C594 | Ho1112ac |

**March 1916**

| 04159 | *Bric-à-Brac.* 'The Optimist and the Pessimist' | | |
|---|---|---|---|
| | ('Up-to-date' version w. Nelson Keys) | CR C667 | Ho630af |

**December 1916**

| 04188 | *Vanity Fair.* 'The Tory and the Rad' | | |
|---|---|---|---|
| | (w. Stanley Logan) | CR C761 | Ho2416af |

# ELLALINE TERRISS

Ellaline Terriss (1871-1971) was born in the Falkland Islands. At the beginning of her career she appeared in Beerbohm Tree's company and Charles Wyndham's company.

She took one singing lesson from Geraldine Ulmar (the original Elsie Maynard and Gianetta at the Savoy). Miss Ulmar sent her home saying, "No, no, I cannot teach you. That little catch in your voice – that trick of catching your breath – that is you. To take them away would spoil you."

Ellaline Terriss played primarily in straight plays until she appeared as Jessie Bond's sister in *His Excellency*. She then became a star of the Gaiety, appearing in *The Shop Girl, The Circus Girl,* and *A Runaway Girl.* Thereafter she played many more leads on the London stage, and subsequently toured the Music Halls with her husband Seymour Hicks. Late in her career, she appeared in films.

**Black G & T, 1903**

| 03000 | *Blue Bell in Fairyland.* 'I Want Yer, Ma Honey' | | |
|---|---|---|---|
| | | [? May 1903] | 140R |
| | | | (later c) |
| 03001 | ''Tis Only You' | [? May 1903] | 142R |
| | | | (later c) |
| 03006 | 'Gaiety Medley' | [June 1903] | 218R |
| | | | (later c) |
| GC3440 | *The Circus Girl.* 'Just a Little Piece of String' | CR | 3700b |
| GC3441 | 'Louisiana Lou' | | 3702b |
| GC3457 | 'Gaiety Medley' | [26 June 1903] | 3955b |

**(continued over)**

**Ellaline Terriss (cont.)**

**Black G & T, 1907-8**

| GC3678 | 'My Indiana Anna' | [29 January 1907] | 9893b |
|---|---|---|---|
| GC3705 | 'Glow Little Glow Worm' | [29 January 1907] | 9895b |
| GC3741 | The Gay Gordons. 'Humpty and Dumpty' | CR | 7545e |
| GC3742 | The Gay Gordons. 'Everybody Loves Me' | CR | 7550e |

Ellaline Terriss made an equal number of unissued records about the same time. She made a few electrics in the early 1930s, almost forty years after she worked with Gilbert.

# GEORGE GROSSMITH, JR.

George Grossmith, Jr. (1874-1935) came from a theatrical family. He was the brother of Lawrence Grossmith, the nephew of Weedon Grossmith. He was the son of George Grossmith (1847-1912), the original Ko-Ko, and principal comedian at the Opera Comique and the Savoy until 1889.

It may be stretching a point to include George, Jr. in this discography, however, his place here rests on two appearances. In 1893 he made his début in the role of Young Foodle in Haste to the Wedding by Gilbert, with music by Grossmith Sr. In 1902 he appeared as the Usher in Trial by Jury in a charity matinée performance at the Lyric Theatre. Rutland Barrington was the Judge. Both productions were under Gilbert's direction. "Gilbert was kindness itself to me," George Grossmith, Jr. wrote in his memoirs, "though he seemed to terrify my father."

Grossmith, Jr. appeared in Morocco Bound with music by Osmond Carr, and the original production of A Gaiety Girl, and subsequently became a major star of the Gaiety Theatre under the management of George Edwardes. He made several tours of America. He co-authored more than a dozen West End productions and appeared in such non-musical plays as The Gay Lord Quex, The Admirable Crighton, and The Critic. His theatrical career lasted forty years.

George Grossmith, Jr. made about forty recordings, all of Variety and musical comedy numbers. One song, however, comes within the scope of this survey, 'The Two Obediahs'. The earliest version of this song was written in the 1880s when it was frequently sung by the comedian J.L. Toole, the star of Thespis. Gilbert used a few verses of 'The Two Obediahs' at the beginning of the third act of his play, Engaged.

The lyrics were re-written from time to time. An 'up-to-date' version was sung by George Grossmith and Teddy Payne on the closing night of the old Gaiety Theatre in 1903. The version which they recorded, however, was written after 1910, for the last verse refers to Thomas Beecham's production of *Salomé*(!) which was produced in that year for the first time at Covent Garden.

**March 1911**

| 04085 | 'The Two Obediahs' | | |
|---|---|---|---|
| | (Geo. Grossmith and Edmund Payne) | C567 | z4916f |

## THE TWENTIETH CENTURY

Arthur Sullivan died in November of 1900; Queen Victoria in January 1901, and Richard D'Oyly Carte in April of that year. The new century brought with it many changes. Mrs. D'Oyly Carte kept the Savoy company together as long as she could. But with Sullivan dead and Gilbert in virtual retirement, and with the rising popularity of a new theatrical genre called musical comedy, Helen D'Oyly Carte made the painful decision to disband the London company in the spring of 1903. Many of the principals, including Henry Lytton, Walter Passmore, Robert Evett, and Louie Pounds, went into the cast of *The Earl and the Girl* at the Adelphi, and made good careers for themselves in West End musicals. Rosina Brandram appeared in *Veronique* (with Ruth Vincent) the following year. Only Henry Lytton ever returned permanently to Gilbert and Sullivan.

The gramophone companies did relatively little recording from the operas when the D'Oyly Carte Company was absent from London. Three and a half years later, however, Mrs. D'Oyly Carte formed a new company, and produced a season of four operas at the Savoy (1906-7) with Gilbert coming out of retirement to direct. It was highly successful, and a second London season was produced in 1908-9. The leading comedian of these seasons was Charles Workman, who leased the Savoy himself for the 1909-10 season and produced three new operas, including *Fallen Fairies* by W.S. Gilbert and Edward German.

It was in this time-frame that Leo Sheffield, Bertha Lewis, and Sydney Granville got their earliest training in Gilbert and Sullivan operas. During these years also J.M. Gordon first assumed the duties of stage manager.

It was J.M. Gordon (who became Stage Director of the D'Oyly Carte Company in 1912) together with Henry Lytton, Bertha Lewis, Leo Sheffield, and Sydney Granville, who carried Gilbert's traditions well into the twentieth century. The next section of this book details the recordings that were made by singers who appeared at the Savoy Theatre during the London seasons of 1906-10 while Gilbert was still active.

Richard Green in *The Gondoliers*, 1907.
(Courtesy of the Ray Mander and Joe Mitchenson Theatre Collection)

## RICHARD GREEN

Richard Green (1870-1914) made his début in *Ivanhoe* at Sullivan's ill-fated Royal English Opera, and subsequently appeared in *Haddon Hall* at the Savoy. He appeared at Covent Garden the following season, and was Silvio in the English première of *I Pagliacci*. He also played Escamillo at Drury Lane, and Konrad in *Die Meistersinger* at Covent Garden with Jean de Reske [1895]. He was seen in *The French Maid* by Basil Hood and Walter Slaughter, and a few other West End musicals, and made his last appearance at the Savoy as Giuseppe in the 1907 revival of *The Gondoliers*.

(continued over)

**Richard Green (cont.)**

|         | **Black G & T, 1901**                         |        |
| ------- | --------------------------------------------- | ------ |
| GC2409  | 'Two Little Irish Songs' (Löhr)               | 973b   |
| GC2410  | 'A Song of Thanksgiving' (Allitson)           | 974b   |
| GC2411  | 'The Devout Lover' (White)                    | 949b   |

|          | **8 November 1904** (10")                            |          |
| -------- | ---------------------------------------------------- | -------- |
| unissued | 'At My Lady's Feet'                                  | 6215b    |
| unissued | 'Thy Throne'                                         | 6216b    |
| unissued | 'Tis the Day' ['Mattinata'] Leoncavallo              | 6217-8b  |
| unissued | Prologue [*Pagliacci*?]                              | 6219b    |

# HAROLD WILDE

Harold Wilde was the principal tenor with the D'Oyly Carte Company in the 1906-7 season in which he played the Duke of Dunstable, Frederick, Earl Tolloller and Marco, all under Gilbert's direction. For more than ten years he was in the Gramophone Company's stable of recording artists, and he frequently appeared in recordings of 'Gems' from this and that, the odd quartet or male chorus, generally without credit on the record label. Before the First World War he made a large number of recordings under his own name for the Gramophone Company's lower priced Green Zonophone Label. He recorded about fifty English popular songs and ballads including the following Gilbert and Sullivan items.

|      | **Double-sided Green Zonophone, c. September 1910**           |          |
| ---- | ------------------------------------------------------------ | -------- |
| 313  | *The Gondoliers*. 'Take a Pair of Sparkling Eyes'            | 12126e   |

|      | **July 1912**                                    |           |
| ---- | ------------------------------------------------ | --------- |
| 891  | *The Yeomen of the Guard*. 'Is Life a Boon?'    | Ab15394e  |
| 891  | *The Mikado*. 'A Wand'ring Minstrel I'          | Ab15396e  |

|      | **November 1912**                                            |          |
| ---- | ------------------------------------------------------------ | -------- |
| 1003 | *The Yeomen of the Guard*. 'Free From His Fetters Grim'      | y16058e  |
| 1003 | *The Pirates of Penzance*.                                   |          |
|      | 'Oh, Is there not one Maiden Breast?'                        | y16057e  |

Harold Wilde sang in the chorus of the following complete acoustic recordings:
1921 *Patience*
1922 *Iolanthe*
1923 *H.M.S. Pinafore*
1925 *Princess Ida*

# STRAFFORD MOSS

Strafford Moss appeared at the Savoy as the Defendant in the 1898 revival of *Trial By Jury*. In 1903 he was featured in a matinée performance of *Bob*, an opera by François Cellier and Cunningham Bridgeman. In 1908 he played Nanki-Poo in *The Mikado* at the Savoy. The same season he appeared in *A Welsh Sunset* with Bertha Lewis and Leo Sheffield which was playing in repertory with *H.M.S. Pinafore* at the Savoy. He was principal tenor with the D'Oyly Carte touring company from 1906 to 1914. His only known recordings are these two duets from *The Naughty Princess*.

**Columbia, 1920**

| | | | |
|---|---|---|---|
| F1064 | *The Naughty Princess.* 'What We'll Do' (w. George Grossmith, Jr.) | CR | 74210-2 |
| F1064 | *The Naughty Princess.* 'Hush! Hush! (w. George Grossmith, Jr.) | CR | 74211-2 |

# ELSIE SPAIN

Elsie Spain made her début in *Miss Hook of Holland* (replacing Isabel Jay) in 1907. The following season she was principal soprano at the Savoy. There she made a favourable impression upon Charles Workman who wanted to cast her as the Fairy Queen in Gilbert's last opera *Fallen Fairies*. Gilbert, however, insisted on casting Nancy McIntosh.

Miss Spain subsequently appeared in *The Chocolate Soldier* (with Charles Workman) and *The Quaker Girl* and continued to appear in West End shows until 1916. Thereafter she toured in Variety. She is known to have made only one recording, presumably at Workman's invitation.

**Odeon, 1910**

| | |
|---|---|
| 0743 | *The Yeomen of the Guard.* 'I Have a Song to Sing Oh' (w. Ch. Workman) |

Amy Evans, the last of the Savoyards, in A Waltz Dream

## AMY EVANS

Amy Evans (1884-1983) was the daughter of a Welsh coal miner. She won the singing competition in the Cardiff Eidsteddfod of 1899. This was the beginning of a professional singing career which lasted seventy-seven years.

She was a member of Charles Workman's company at the Savoy in 1910 and understudy to Nancy McIntosh whom she replaced at the end of the first week in Fallen Fairies. She subsequently pursued a concert career, married the Scottish baritone Fraser Gange, and settled in America. She last sang in public for the Welsh Women's Clubs of America at the age of 91!

She made a few recordings for the English Pathé Company and Edison Bell (cylinders). They are never encountered.

Amy Evans, the last of the Savoyards, died at her home in Baltimore, Maryland, in January 1983 at the age of 98.

**Edison Bell Cylinders, 1906** (Welsh Series)

| | |
|---|---|
| 14202 | 'Y Deryn Pur' |
| 14208 | *Blodwen*. 'Hywel a Blodwen' (w. John Roberts) (Joseph Parry) |
| 14209 | 'Llam y Cariadau' (R.S. Hughes) |

**Pathé Etched Label Discs, 1906-7**

| | |
|---|---|
| 60543 | *Theodora*. 'Angels Ever Bright and Fair' (Handel) |
| 60564 | *Faust*. Trio (w. Bantock Pierpoint, Alfred Heather) |
| 77114 | *The Country Girl*. 'Boy and Girl' (w. Francis Ludlow) |
| 77115 | *Veronique*. 'The Donkey Duet' (w. Francis Ludlow) |
| 77116 | *Veronique*. 'The Swing Song' (w. Francis Ludlow) |
| 77117 | *The Cingalee*. 'You and I' (w. Francis Ludlow) |

See Complete Sets: The Yeomen of the Guard, Pathé


# CLAUDE FLEMING

Claude Fleming (1884-1952) was born in Australia where he acted from 1903 to 1906. On his way to England he appeared in *Sweet Nell of Old Drury* in San Fransisco and *Lady Madcap* in New York. On his arrival in London he appeared with Beerbohm Tree's company. His next engagement was in *The Mastersingers* at Covent Garden.

In 1910 he appeared in *Fallen Fairies* with Leo Sheffield and Charles Workman. Thereafter he appeared in a large number of musicals. The only recordings he is known to have made were from *A Southern Maid* (the show in which Martyn Green made his début). In 1927 Claude Fleming began a film career and appeared in several Hollywood movies.

**Columbia, 1920**

| | | | |
|---|---|---|---|
| F1054 | *A Southern Maid*. 'The Call of the Sea' | CR | 74126 |
| F1054 | *A Southern Maid*. 'I Want the Sun and the Moon' (w. José Collins) | CR | 74127 |
| F1055 | *A Southern Maid*. 'Here's to those We Love' | CR | 74128 |

## LEO SHEFFIELD

Leo Sheffield (1873-1951) made his début playing small parts in the 1906-7 season at the Savoy. He played Luiz and Private Willis among other roles in the 1908-9 season. Gilbert liked him and cast him in *Fallen Fairies* in 1910.

Sheffield spent the next ten years touring in *The Chocolate Soldier*, *The Girl in the Taxi*, *The Laughing Husband*, among others. From 1919 to 1930 he played most of Rutland Barrington's roles with the D'Oyly Carte Company. Thereafter he appeared in West End revivals of *The Geisha* and *San Toy* (in which Barrington had also appeared). Leo Sheffield appeared in several pantomimes and was a member of the BBC Drama Company.

He recorded all of the roles for which he was famous with the exception of Captain Corcoran in *H.M.S. Pinafore* and Private Willis in *Iolanthe*. A curiosity is his only known non-Gilbert and Sullivan recording: a duet with Cicely Courtneidge, from the film *Falling for You* which he made after he left the D'Oyly Carte Company.

|  | **23 February 1915** |  |
|---|---|---|
| unissued | 'Laughing Song' (Darnley/Pink) |  |
|  | **HMV, November 1919** |  |
| unissued | *The Gondoliers.* 'There Lived a King' | Ho5407ae |
|  | **HMV, 1931** |  |
| B4475 | 'Mrs. Bartholomew' (w. Cicely Courtneidge) | 30-10834 |

Leo Sheffield appeared in the following complete recordings for the Gramophone Company:

| 1924 | *Ruddigore.* Sir Despard |
|---|---|
| 1925 | *Princess Ida.* King Hildebrand |
| 1926 | *The Mikado.* Pooh-Bah |
| 1927 | *The Gondoliers.* Don Alhambra |
| 1928 | *Trial by Jury.* The Learned Judge |
| 1929 | *The Yeomen of the Guard.* Wilfred Shadbolt |
| 1929 | *The Pirates of Penzance.* Sergeant of Police |

See Complete Recordings, p. 90

# BERTHA LEWIS

Bertha Lewis (1887-1931) was educated at the Ursuline Convent in Upton. She made her first stage appearance in a D'Oyly Carte touring company in 1906. She made her London début in *A Welsh Sunset* at the Savoy in 1908, and was in the Gilbert and Sullivan season in London, 1908-9.

Between 1909 and 1914 she made concert tours of the United Kingdom, and appeared as Carmen, Amneris in *Aida*, and Dalila. In 1912 she made a number of recordings for the Gramophone Company of 'Gems' from popular musicals. [She was not credited on the labels.] She rejoined the D'Oyly Carte Company in 1914 and was their principal contralto from then until her death. She died tragically in a car accident in 1931.

Bertha Lewis recorded all of her famous roles with the exception of Lady Sangazure in *The Sorcerer*, (most of) Ruth in *The Pirates of Penzance*, and Dame Carruthers in *The Yeomen of the Guard*. She had already died when the D'Oyly Carte Company recorded *The Sorcerer* for the first time, and she was on tour in America in 1928 when *The Pirates of Penzance* and *The Yeomen of the Guard* were recorded. A copy of her 1920 test from *The Yeomen of the Guard* has not turned up.

Bertha Lewis appeared in the following recordings of 'Gems' for His Master's Voice in 1912. She may have appeared on other records in this series.

| | | | | |
|---|---|---|---|---|
| 04529-30 | *The Sunshine Girl.* | 11/7/12 | C522 | 6313-4f |
| 04531-2 | *Princess Caprice.* | 13/8/12 | | 6463-4f |
| 04534 | *Florodora.* | 18/7/12 | C516 | 6532f |
| 04535 | *The Duchess of Danzig.* | 8/12 | C516 | 6468f |
| 04550 | *Gypsy Love.* [trans. Basil Hood] | 12/12 | C518 | 6884f |

**November 1919**

| | | | |
|---|---|---|---|
| unissued | 'When Our Gallant Norman foes' | (12") | Ho4124af |

Bertha Lewis appeared in the following complete recordings for the Gramophone Company:

| | |
|---|---|
| 1922 | *H.M.S. Pinafore.* Little Buttercup |
| 1924 | *Ruddigore.* Dame Hannah |
| 1925 | *Princess Ida.* Lady Blanche* |
| 1926 | *The Mikado.* Katisha |
| 1927 | *The Gondoliers.* Duchess of Plaza-Toro |
| 1930 | *Iolanthe.* Queen of the Fairies |
| 1930 | *H.M.S. Pinafore.* Little Buttercup |
| 1930 | *Patience.* Lady Jane |
| 1931 | *The Pirates of Penzance.* Ruth (Abridged)   See Complete Recordings, p. 90 |

*Bertha Lewis sings 'Come Mighty Must' in this recording.

## SYDNEY GRANVILLE

Sydney Granville (1880-1959) appeared with the Moody Manners Company before joining the D'Oyly Carte Company in 1907. In 1908 he was the Boatswain in the revival of *H.M.S. Pinafore* at the Savoy. He toured with the D'Oyly Carte Company until 1914, and rejoined the Company after the war. He played light baritone roles – Giuseppe, Strephon, Pish-Tush, Grosvenor, etc. – until 1925 when he toured for two years in Australia. He returned to England in 1927 and appeared in *The Blue Train* and *The Beggar's Opera*. He rejoined the D'Oyly Carte Company in 1928 and became successor to Leo Sheffield.

Sydney Granville recorded a few of his early light baritone roles acoustically and all of the heavy baritone roles electrically with the exception of the Judge in *Trial by Jury* and (inexplicably) King Hildebrand in *Princess Ida*.

He remained with the Company until 1941. Sydney Granville appeared in the colour film of *The Mikado* in 1938.

Sydney Granville appeared in the following complete recordings for the Gramophone Company

| | |
|---|---|
| 1922 | *Iolanthe.* Strephon |
| 1922 | *H.M.S. Pinafore.* Captain Corcoran* |
| | The Boatswain |
| 1925 | *Princess Ida.* Florian |
| 1930 | *Iolanthe.* Private Willis |
| 1930 | *H.M.S. Pinafore.* The Boatswain |
| 1931 | *The Yeomen of the Guard.* Wilfred Shadbolt (Abridged) |
| 1931 | *The Pirates of Penzance.* Sergeant of Police (Abridged) |
| 1931 | *The Gondoliers.* Don Alhambra (Abridged) |
| 1931 | *Ruddigore.* Sir Despard |
| 1936 | *The Mikado.* Pooh-Bah |

See Complete Recordings, p. 90
See *The Mikado*, film, p. 92

*Sydney Granville never appeared in this role onstage.

*By stretching a point it is possible to include the following two artists in this survey.*

## JULIUS LIEBAN

Julius Lieban (1857-1948) was a tenor buffo with the Berlin Opera from 1882 to 1912. His specialty was Mime in Wagner's *Ring*, a role which he sang under Mahler at Covent Garden in 1892, and again with Jean de Reszke in1897.

"A small but useful tenor," Sullivan wrote in his diary, when he heard Lieban sing in 1893. Sullivan chose him for the role of deBracy in the German production of *Ivanhoe*. The opera was produced in Berlin under Sullivan's supervision in 1895.

Herr Lieban made several recordings of German opera and operetta. He recorded only one Gilbert and Sullivan song – four times. It gives us another interesting look at nineteenth century traditions.[*]

|  | **Berlin G & T, 1902** |  |
|---|---|---|
| GC2-42598 | *Der Mikado*. 'Bachstelzenlied' [Tit Willow] | 1507XA2 |
|  | **Berlin Odeon, 1905** |  |
| 34502 | *Der Mikado*. 'Bachstelzenlied' [Tit Willow] |  |
|  | **Edison Bell Cylinder, 1905** |  |
| 15069 | *Der Mikado*. 'Bachstelzenlied' [Tit Willow] |  |
|  | **Berlin G & T, 1907** |  |
| GC3-42820 | *Der Mikado*. 'Bachstelzenlied' [Tit Willow] | 2959r |

[*]See also p. 31, note.

## LILIAN RUSSELL

Lillian Russell (1851-1922) at the beginning of her career, played the title role in *Patience,* and Aline in *The Sorcerer* in New York in 1882 and 1883. In the summer of 1883 she went to London and played Virginia in *Virginia and Paul.* She remained there to play the title roles in *Polly* and *Pocahontas.* Some of her performances were seen by Gilbert and Sullivan, and she was subsequently engaged to play the title role in *Princess Ida.*

Miss Russell, however, was not aware that there were no 'stars' at the Savoy, and she quickly angered Gilbert by missing two rehearsals. "I will not work with her," said Gilbert. Miss Russell had one of the shortest careers at the Savoy. Gilbert insisted that she be dismissed. Her attorney insisted that she had a contract, and Gilbert insisted that her contract "required her to attend rehearsals." Miss Russell was then allowed to "withdraw" from her contract on the grounds that her health would not permit her to attend rehearsals.

She returned to America where she starred for the next twenty-five years in operetta (many by Offenbach) and musical comedy. She was Teresa in the New York production of *The Mountebanks.* She was married (for a while) to the English composer, Edward Solomon.

Her only known recording is an unreleased Columbia (which survives in a test pressing) of 1912. The song, 'Come Down, Ma Evenin Star' is from the 1902 American musical *Twirly Whirly.* The composer, John Stromberg, died during the rehearsals, and the manuscript of the song was found in his hotel room after his death. It had consequently great sentimental value for Miss Russell who sang it frequently during the remainder of her career.

**Columbia, 1912**

| | | |
|---|---|---|
| unissued | 'Come Down, Ma Evening Star' | 19830-1 |

## THE GERMAN REED ENTERTAINMENTS

Before Gilbert and Sullivan wrote *Trial by Jury*, or even *Thespis* for that matter, they both worked, on a much more modest scale, at Mr and Mrs German Reed's Gallery of Illustration in Regent Street. Started in 1856, the 'gallery' did not call itself a theatre because in the 1850s the theatre was still not altogether respectable.

Productions at the Gallery of Illustration were modest. A piano and harmonium generally provided all the musical accompaniment, and a cast of six performers was about as elaborate as a production could get. Under these conditions, operas by Gilbert and Clay, Sullivan and Burnand, Charles Stephenson and Alfred Cellier, and even George Grossmith, were produced.

The performers included German Reed, Mrs German Reed, Sullivan's friend Arthur Cecil, Fanny Holland, and a comedian with the unlikely name of Corney Grain. Richard Corney Grain appeared in the operas, wrote a number of sketches, and frequently performed at the piano in the traditions of the nineteenth century entertainer.

Corney Grain died in 1895, the year in which the German Reed establishment finally ended. Some of his songs, however, were recorded a few years later by Louis Bradfield.

Louis Bradfield (1844-1919) was a popular star of West End musicals at the turn of the century (*The Gaiety Girl, The Geisha, Florodora*). He had ample opportunity to see Corney Grain in person. His recordings of Corney Grain's material have an indelible ring of authenticity. They are unusual contemporary interpretations of the all-but-lost nineteenth century 'topical song', and they form a unique link with the theatrical traditions in which both Gilbert and Sullivan served their apprenticeship.

The following recordings are of Louis Bradfield performing Corney Grain material.

|  | **March 1902** |  |  |
|---|---|---|---|
| GC2-2641 | 'The Polka and the Choir Boy' |  | 1561b |
|  | **2 March 1905** |  |  |
| 3-2584 | 'My First Cigar' | (7″) | 904d |
| GC3-2245 | 'My First Cigar' |  | 1873e |
| Zon X42298 | 'The Polka and the Choir Boy' |  | 1875e |

## 'THE ABSENT-MINDED BEGGAR'

The first time the gramophone was used as part of a commercial appeal may well have been during the Boer War, and as early as 1899.

Sullivan wrote the song, 'The Absent-Minded Beggar' to words by Rudyard Kipling. He finished it on 5 November 1899. It was orchestrated by George Byng* and sung by John Coates at the Alhambra on 13 November with Sullivan conducting. On 22 or 23 November another singer, Ian Colquhoun, recorded it. Colquhoun was known as 'the iron-voiced baritone' and was a popular singer of patriotic songs. On 21 December 1899, the following announcement appeared in the Daily Mail:

> IAN COLQUHOUN has generously sung for us SIR A. SULLIVAN'S Musical Setting of RUDYARD KIPLING'S Celebrated Poem. IT IS CLEAR, LOUD, AND DISTINCTLY ENUNCIATED. The song required two discs for the reproduction, and is sold in complete sets only. The total receipts from the sale of these records at the full price, 5s. are to be forwarded by us to the Daily Mail War Fund.

Over four thousand sets of these records were sold in 1900, and £1,000 was thus collected for War Relief. This is one of the few recordings of a Sullivan song that Sullivan could have heard.

| | | | |
|---|---|---|---|
| A | Ian Colquhoun: 'The Absent-Minded Beggar', verses 1 & 2 | | |
| | | AX, AXX, etc.** | |
| B | Ian Colquhoun: 'The Absent-Minded Beggar', verses 3 & 4 | | |
| | | BX, BXX, etc. | |

Six months later the song was recorded without a soloist.

| | | | |
|---|---|---|---|
| 115 | Municipal Military Orchestra: | | |
| | 'The Absent-Minded Beggar' | [11 June 1900] | 4523 |

*George Byng was the Music Director for the Gramophone Company in the early 1920s. He conducted four of the acoustic recordings of the Savoy operas, 1917-1922. See p. 89-90.

**This was an out-of-series record using the letters 'A' and 'B' instead of catalogue numbers. Because so many copies were pressed, several matrices were used with out-of-series matrix numbers AX, AXX, etc.

# BAND RECORDINGS

In the early days of recording, Fred Gaisberg learned that nothing reproduced better by the zinc or wax process that the sound of a small band. As a result, band and instrumental music figured prominently in the repertoire of the Gramophone Company's 7″ catalogue.

As early as the autumn of 1898, instrumental records of Gilbert and Sullivan began to appear.

**18 September 1898**

| | |
|---|---|
| E554 | *The Gondoliers.* Selection I  Trocadero Orchestra |
| E557 | *The Mikado.* Selection I  Trocadero Orchestra |
| E558 | *The Mikado.* Selection II Trocadero Orchestra |

**October 1898**

| | |
|---|---|
| 8017 | 'Brightly Dawns our Wedding Day' |
| | Fransella's Flute Quartet |

The last item was re-numbered and issued under catalogue number 9153.
The above recordings were made before the introduction of serial matrix numbers.

In 1899 the first systematic attempt was made to present the music of Gilbert and Sullivan on record in England. That a series of seventeen 7″ records should have been made in the nineteenth century only attests to the incredible popularity of the operas at the time. Judging from the number of copies of these recordings still in existence, they must have sold very well. In fact, sides from this series were recorded over and over as the masters wore out. Before 1900, a 7″ master could be expected to produce about 500 copies of a record. Replacement recordings were issued under the old catalogue numbers with added suffix letters (eg. 32X, 32Z, 32W, 32Y, in that order) to indicate a substitution. When a substitution occurred, the matrix number of course was different.

**Royal Artillery Band, October 1899**

| | | |
|---|---|---|
| 31 | *The Mikado.* Introduction of Act II* | 3966 |
| 32 | *The Mikado.* Selection II | 3968 |
| 33 | 'The Flowers that Bloom in the Spring' | 3969 |
| 34 | Finale to *The Mikado* | 3970 |
| 35 | Chorus of Police from *Patience* (sic!) | 3962 |
| 36 | 'The Soldiers of our Queen' *and* 'Bunthorne's Song' | 3957 |
| 37 | 'The Policeman's Song' *and* 'The Modern Major General' | 3961 |
| 38 | 'I Hear the Soft Voice' (sic) *and* | |
| | 'When I First Put this Uniform On' | 3958 |

Number 39 is not a Gilbert and Sullivan selection.
*Actually 'Behold the Lord High Executioner'

| 40 | 'Let's Give Three Cheers' and 'When I was a Lad' | 3964 |
|----|--------------------------------------------------|------|
| 41 | 'Little Buttercup' | 3963 |
| 42 | 'For He Himself Has Said It' and | |
|    | 'Never Mind the Why and Wherefore' | 3965 |
| 43 | 'Take a Pair of Sparkling Eyes' | 3975 |
| 44 | Gavotte [The Gondoliers] | 3976 |
| 45 | 'No Possible Doubt Whatever' and Cachucha | 3978 |
| 46 | The Gondoliers. Selection II | 3974 |
| 76 | Iolanthe. Selection | 3980 |
| 77 | The Gondoliers. Selection I | 4056 |

The titles above are listed as they appear on the records.

All of the above matrix numbers belong to the early 'unlettered' series.

It is interesting to note that as early as 28 November 1899 record number 32 was replaced by 32X [matrix 4347]. Five selections were re-recorded in May 1901. As late as December 1903 a new series of seventeen 7" records by the Coldstream Guards was commenced. By this date, however, the 12" record had been introduced, and the new 7" records received little if any distribution.

There was little other music by Sullivan recorded on 7" records aside from 'Onward Christian Soldiers' [E4056, 9312] and 'The Lost Chord' [E8022, 5051, 5052]. However Sullivan's last completed opera, *The Rose of Persia*, which closed in June of 1900, received some contemporary attention from the gramophone.*

**Municipal Military Orchestra**

| 111 | The Rose of Persia. 'Drinking Song' and Finale | 11/6/00 | 4521 |
|-----|-----------------------------------------------|---------|------|
| 111X | The Rose of Persia. 'Drinking Song' and Finale | 23/3/01 | 2830a |

**Municipal Orchestra, 28 November 1900**

| 674 | The Rose of Persia. Lancers Figure I | 1668B(a) |
|-----|--------------------------------------|----------|
| 675 | The Rose of Persia. Lancers Figure II | 1669B(a) |
| 676 | The Rose of Persia. Lancers Figure III-IV | 1670B(a) |
| 677 | The Rose of Persia. Lancers Figure V | 1671B(a) |

When 10" records came into general use in 1901, they were used for only a small number of Gilbert and Sullivan band recordings. It was in 1903, however, when the 12" records were released, that instrumental arrangements of music from the popular operas began to be issued in ever-increasing numbers. These selections continued to be recorded during the

*A contemporary catalogue of Edisonia, Ltd. (cylinders) lists three items from *The Rose of Persia*:
140     Selection I. 'With Martial Gait', 'The Small Street Arab', 'Time Will Soften Every Man'.
141     Selection II. 'Try to Forget' (Cornet solo).
142     Selection III. 'The Drinking Song', Finale and March.

electric era. While they sold well and are still commonly met with, they are of generally little interest although a few of the band recordings issued in the early days merit some consideration.

**30 May 1903**

| 08 | *The Emerald Isle.* London Regimental Band | | | |
|---|---|---|---|---|

**The Coldstream Guards**

| 0151 | *Henry VIII.* 'Graceful Dance' | 1908 | C235 | 2305f |
|---|---|---|---|---|
| 0183 | *Haddon Hall* | 1908 | | 2750f |
| 0201 | *Henry VIII.* 'Graceful Dance' | 1909 | | 2950f |
| 0256 | *Utopia, (Limited)* | 1910 | C235 | 4076f |
| 0270 | *The Golden Legend.* 'Evening Hymn' | 1910 | | 4039f |
| 0311 | *Ivanhoe* | 1910 | C103 | 4027f |
| 0328 | *Haddon Hall* | 1911 | C105 | 5298f |
| 0333 | 'The Long Day Closes' | 1911 | C248 | 5296f |
| 2079-80 | *The Emerald Isle* | 1915 | C415 | AL8312-3f |

The 'Graceful Dance' from Sullivan's Incidental Music to *Henry VIII* served as the original Overture to *The Sorcerer* in 1877. A double-sided arrangement of *Utopia, (Limited)* was issued by Vocalion, K05072, and a Zonophone arrangement of *The Sorcerer,* A322, includes the melody 'Happy Are We'.

One more unusual band recording is worthy of note. Arthur Sullivan was at Nauheim in the autumn of 1896. A note in his Diary on 22 September reads:

> After dinner we went to the Kursaal to see a conjurer... Band played a capital march by Komçak, 'Barataria' made on themes from *The Gondoliers*.

This curiosity was recorded several times in the early days of recording in Germany.

**Barataria Marsch**

| 40049 | Garde Fuselier Regt. January 1900 | | (7″) | 384A |
|---|---|---|---|---|
| 40113 | 3 Garde Grenadier Regt. zu Fuss, Berlin 1901 | | (7″) | 23B |
| | | | | (later a) |
| GC40399 | Kaiser Alexander Garde-Grenadier Regt. 1903 | | | 1605h |
| Z-20527 | Seidler's Orch. c. 1905 | | [Zon] | |
| 020530 | Seidler's Orch. c. 1905 | | [5″ Zon] | |

## MECHANICAL MUSIC

Mechanical music was extremely popular before the introduction of the gramophone. Barrel organs, music boxes, player pianos and disc music boxes were available in great variety, and the music of Gilbert and Sullivan was the most popular fare.

Most of the mechanical programmes were of little individual interest. However, there were a few years around the turn of the century when the music box manufacturers began to take a serious interest in the theatre in the West End of London. All of a sudden it was possible to buy arrangements of as many as ten different songs from shows like *Florodora*, *The Geisha*, and *A Runaway Girl* for use on disc music boxes. The demand for mechanical music of course, ended quickly once the gramophone established itself. But before it did, a series of five excerpts from *The Emerald Isle* became available on nineteen ⅝" Polyphon discs. *The Emerald Isle* was Sullivan's last opera, completed by Edward German, and produced at the Savoy Theatre in 1901.

**Music Box Discs, c. 1901**

| | |
|---|---|
| 50426 | *The Emerald Isle.* 'If You Wish to Appear' |
| 50427 | *The Emerald Isle.* 'When Alfred's Friends' |
| 50428 | *The Emerald Isle.* 'Oh, Setting Sun' |
| 50429 | *The Emerald Isle.* 'Oh Have You Met' |
| 50430 | *The Emerald Isle.* 'Oh the Age in Which We're Living' |

## THE FIRST COMPLETE RECORDINGS

When the D'Oyly Carte Opera Company returned to the Savoy in December of 1906 after an absence of three and a half years, the Gramophone Company was thrown into a flurry of activity, recording Gilbert and Sullivan with all the wrong people. Something called the 'Sullivan Operatic Party' began to record bits of the more popular operas in July of 1906. The Sullivan Operatic Party was a name used to mean whoever was in the studio that day.

While members of the 'original casts' occasionally recorded during the first decade of this century, the Gramophone Company preferred to record with its own stable of gramophone artists whose voices they felt recorded well. The Sullivan Operatic Party, for example, included singers like Peter Dawson, Eleanor Jones-Hudson, Ernest Pike and Stanley Kirkby.

Often a gramophone artist would know in advance that he was to record excerpts from a current musical, and he would go to the show in question to hear how a song was presented. Just as often, however, the artist would walk into the studio, pick up a piece of music which he had never seen before, and record it at the same session. Much of the work of the Sullivan Operatic Party sounds as if it had been done under the latter conditions.

The Sullivan Operatic Party was responsible for two sets of more or less complete recordings that appeared in 1906 and 1907. Most of *The Yeomen of the Guard* (including the Overture) could be obtained on nineteen single-sided records. And most of *The Mikado* was available on seventeen single-sided records. These recordings, however, had not been made systematically, and the casts were not consistent. They were intended to be purchased individually, and they were. The idea to market them as 'complete' sets was an afterthought.

When the London production of *The Mikado* was banned during the 1907 State visit of Prince Fushimi of Japan, the Gramophone Company was quick to capitalize on the event. The records of *The Mikado* suddenly became available as a complete package at a special price, and a publicity campaign was launched, urging the public to go to their local record store and hear the "banned opera"! What is more, the Gramophone Company presented a copy of the recording to Mr K. Sugimura (who was attached to the Prince). His appreciation of the records was announced in a full-page advertisement in *Talking Machine News*: "...of all the presents I have so far received there, they are the most beautiful, the most valuable..."

The Sullivan Operatic Party was also responsible for a series of ten 10″ sides from *H.M.S. Pinafore* which was issued in 1907. These however, stayed in the catalogue only a short time, and were superseded in 1908 when the Gramophone Company issued a complete recording of *H.M.S. Pinafore* on eighteen single-sided records. This was the English branch of the Gramophone Company's first attempt at recording a *complete* opera with a consistent cast. The attempt was successful and is of interest for the performance of Amy Augarde as Little Buttercup and Hebe.

Another series of excerpts from *H.M.S. Pinafore* was issued in the autumn of 1907 by the Russell Hunting Company on eleven 'Gold Moulded' two-minute cylinders. They sold at the bargain price of one shilling each. The singers included Walter Hyde and Harry Dearth. Later in the year, in time for Christmas, the Odeon Company (then allied with the Russell Hunting Company) issued a complete recording of *H.M.S. Pinafore* on ten double-sided discs with largely the same cast. Harry Dearth and Walter Hyde were members of the Odeon Company's stable of recording artists.

A few months later, Odeon issued a complete recording of *The Mikado* which benefited from the performance of Walter Passmore as Ko-Ko. Excellent performances by Harry Dearth and Walter Hyde were assets to both Odeon releases. The Odeon recordings of *H.M.S. Pinafore* and *The Mikado* proved to be far superior to the Gramophone Company's. The singers were better rehearsed, and had more of the performing style of the day. The public, however, was not interested in buying a complete recording of anything in 1908, and complete copies of the Odeon albums are practically non-existent today, only two or three copies being known.

However, if the Odeon recordings are famous for their rarity, the Pathé recording of *The Yeomen of the Guard,* made in 1907, is legendary, for at the moment a complete copy is not known to exist. Pathé recordings were cut with a vertical (rather than a lateral) groove bed, and required a special pick-up to play. For this reason Pathé's sales tended to be limited, at least in England. While no-one in the present generation is known to have heard the Pathé recording, from the evidence at hand (one double-sided disc from the set turned up recently in a garage in Belgium!) the recording appears to have been a successful and interesting idiomatic performance. The cast included Amy Evans, a soprano who later appeared in Gilbert's last opera, and Bantock Pierpoint, a fine ballad and oratorio singer.

The orchestrations used on all of these sets are not Sullivan's. Some instruments (especially the brasses) were recorded better than others by the acoustic process, and it was customary to re-orchestrate for recording purposes.

*THE MIKADO*
*Gramophone Company, 1906*
One 12" and sixteen 10" single-sided records
with booklet £2.15s.6d.
single records: 12" 5s.6d., 10" 3s.6d.

The cast was given as Sullivan Operatic Party with soloists indicated as follows:

| | | | |
|---|---|---|---|
| GC4606 | 'If you Want to Know Who We Are' | B427 | 8792b |
| 02073 | 'A Wand'ring Minstrel I' . . . . . . . . John Harrison D242 | | 733c |
| GC3-2491 | 'Our Great Mikado' . . . . . . . . . . . Stanley Kirkby B429 | | 8793b |
| GC4403 | 'Behold the Lord High Executioner' | B433 | 3583e |
| GC4407 | 'Three Little Maids from School' . . . . . . . . . . . . . | | |
| | Denise Orme, Amy Augarde, Eleanor Jones-Hudson B431 | | 8682b |
| GC4411 | 'So Please You, Sir' . . . . . . . . . . . . Amy Augarde, | | |
| | Denise Orme, Eleanor Jones-Hudson, | | |
| | Stanley Kirkby B428 | | 8683b |
| GC4414 | 'Were You not to Ko-Ko Plighted' . . . . . . . . . . . | | |
| | Ernest Pike, Eleanor Jones-Hudson B430 | | 8970b |
| GC3663 | 'The Sun Whose Rays' . . . . Eleanor Jones-Hudson B434 | | 8979b |
| GC4605 | 'Brightly Dawns Our Wedding Day' . . . . . . . . . . | | |
| | Amy Augarde, Denise Orme, Ernest Pike, | | |
| | Stanley Kirkby B431 | | 8679b |
| GC4408 | 'Here's a How-de-do' | B432 | 8714b |
| GC4412 | 'Miya Sama' . . . . . . . Amy Augarde, Peter Dawson B427 | | 8716b |
| GC3-2476 | 'A More Humane Mikado' . . . . . . . Peter Dawson B434 | | 8721b |
| GC4409 | 'The Criminal Cried' . . . . . . . . . . . Amy Augarde, | | |
| | Peter Dawson B432 | | 8718b |
| GC4607 | 'See how the Fates' | B428 | 9897b |
| GC4410 | 'The Flowers that Bloom in the Spring' . . . . . . . | | |
| | Ernest Pike, Stanley Kirkby B433 | | 8720b |
| unissued | 'Alone and Yet Alive' . . . . . . . . . . Amy Augarde | | 4791h |
| GC3-2493 | 'Tit Willow' . . . . . . . . . . . . . . . . . Stanley Kirkby B429 | | 8955½b |
| GC4413 | 'There is Beauty in the Bellow of the Blast' . . . . . | | |
| | Amy Augarde, Peter Dawson B430 | | 8724b |

*THE YEOMEN OF THE GUARD*
**Gramophone Company, 1907**
Seventeen 10″ and two 12″ single sided records
with booklet, £3.3s.6d.
single records: 10″ 3s.6d., 12″ 5s.6d.

The cast was given as Sullivan Operatic Party with soloists indicated as follows:

| | | | |
|---|---|---|---|
| 0547 | Overture Bohemian Orchestra | C511 | 1017c |
| GC3701 | 'When Maiden Loves' . . . . . . . . . . . Carrie Tubb | B404 | 9992b |
| GC3703 | 'When Our Gallant Norman Foes' . . . . . . . . . . . . | | |
| | Florence Venning | B404 | 10180b |
| GC4423 | 'Alas I Waver To and Fro'. . . . . . . . . . . . . . . . . . . | | |
| | Florence Venning, Peter Dawson, Ernest Pike | B405 | 9885b |
| GC3-2848 | 'Is Life a Boon?' . . . . . . . . . . . . . . . . . Ernest Pike | B409 | 10073b |
| GC4609 | 'Here's a Man of Jollity' | B405 | 6574b |
| GC4415 | 'I Have a Song to Sing Oh!'. . . . . . . . . . . . . . . . . | | |
| | Eleanor Jones-Hudson, Stanley Kirkby | B406 | 9882b |
| GC4422 | 'How Say you, Maiden' . . . . . . . . . . . . . . . . . . . . . | | |
| | Jones-Hudson, Kirkby, Dawson | B406 | 9880b |
| GC3698 | 'Tis Done! I am a Bride' . . . . Eleanor Jones-Hudson | B407 | 9899b |
| GC3699 | 'Were I Thy Bride'. . . . . . . Eleanor Jones-Hudson | B407 | 10187b |
| GC4416 | 'To Thy Fraternal Care' | B408 | 9981b |
| GC4421 | 'Hereupon We're Both Agreed'. . . . . . . . . . . . . . | | |
| | Peter Dawson, Stanley Kirkby | B408 | 9886b |
| GC3-2847 | 'Free from His Fetters Grim' . . . . . . . . Ernest Pike | B409 | 10072b |
| GC4424 | 'Strange Adventure' | B410 | 9875b |
| GC4610 | 'Like a Ghost his Vigil Keeping' | B410 | 9988b |
| GC4426 | 'A Man Who Would Woo a Fair Maid' | B411 | 9878b |
| GC4425 | 'When a Wooer Goes a Wooing' | B411 | 9877b |
| GC4420 | 'Rapture, Rapture'. . . . . . . . . . . . . . . . . . . . . . . . . | | |
| | Florence Venning, Peter Dawson | B403 | 9989b |
| 04500 | Finale Act II | C511 | 980c |

*H.M.S. PINAFORE*
**Gramophone Company, 1908**
*Complete on fourteen 10″ and four 12″ single-sided records*
*with booklet £3.4s.0d.*
single records: 10″ 3s.6d., 12″ 5s.6d.

Sir Joseph Porter. . . . . . . . . . . . . . . . Alan Turner
Captain Corcoran . . . . . . . . . . . . . . . Thorpe Bates
Ralph Rackstraw. . . . . . . . . . . . . . . . . Ernest Pike
Dick Deadeye. . . . . . . . . . . . . . . . . Peter Dawson
Josephine. . . . . . . . . . . . . . Eleanor Jones-Hudson
Little Buttercup ⎫
⎬ . . . . . . . . . . . . . . Amy Augarde
Hebe ⎭

| | | | |
|---|---|---|---|
| GC4469 | Opening Chorus *and* 'I'm Called Little Buttercup' | B435 | 8846e |
| 04032 | 'The Nightingale' *and* 'A Maiden Fair to See' | C513 | 2520f |
| GC4470 | 'The Captain's Song' | B436 | 8793e |
| GC4471 | 'Sorry Her Lot' | B435 | 8787e |
| GC4472 | 'Over the Bright Blue Sea' | B437 | 8847e |
| GC4473 | 'Now Give Three Cheers' *and* 'When I was a Lad' | B437 | 8777e |
| GC4474 | 'A British Tar' | B438 | 8791e |
| GC4457 | 'Refrain Audacious Tar' | B438 | 6744e |
| 04033-4 | Finale Act I | C514 | 2522f |
| | | | 2543f |
| GC4475 | 'Fair Moon' | B436 | 8788e |
| GC4476 | 'Thing Are Seldom what they Seem' | B439 | 8780e |
| 04035 | 'The Hours Creep on Apace' | C513 | 2527f |
| GC4477 | 'Never Mind the Why and Wherefore' | B439 | 8789e |
| GC4478 | 'King Captain' | B440 | 8795e |
| GC4479 | 'In Uttering a Reprobation' | B440 | 8849e |
| GC4480 | 'Farewell My Own' | B441 | 8779e |
| GC4481 | Finale Act II | B441 | 8851eI |

The recording ends with a chorus of 'Rule Britannia'. It is complete, omitting only the overture, entr' acte, and some of the recits.

### THE YEOMEN OF THE GUARD
**Pathé Company, 1907**
Nine double-sided 11¾″ etched label, vertical-cut records
4s.0d. each

Col. Fairfax........................ Ben Ivor
Sgt. Meryll ................ Bantock Pierpoint
Jack Point................... Francis Ludlow
Wilfred Shadbolt........... Bantock Pierpoint
Elsie Maynard................... Amy Evans
Phoebe Meryll ...... Emily Foxcroft, Amy Evans
Dame Carruthers ............. Emily Foxcroft
With orchestra accompaniment by the Band of H.M. Scots Guards

| | |
|---|---|
| 76086 | 'When Maiden Loves' |
| 76071 | 'When Our Gallant Norman Foes' |
| 76083 | 'Is Life a Boon' |
| 76073 | 'How say you, Maiden' |
| 76085 | 'I've Jibe and Joke' |
| 76087 | 'Were I Thy Bride' |
| 76081 | 'Oh, Sergeant Meryll, is it True?' |
| 76077 | 'Didst Thou not oh Leonard Meryll' |
| 76076 | 'To Thy Fraternal Care' |
| 76070 | 'The Prisoner Comes' |
| 76078 | 'Night has Spread her Pall Once More' |
| 76075 | 'Hereupon we're both Agreed' |
| 76082 | 'Free From his Fetters Grim' |
| 76080 | 'Strange Adventure' |
| 76072 | 'A Man Who Would Woo a Fair Maid' |
| 76074 | 'When a Wooer goes a-wooing' |
| 76079 | 'I Have a Song to Sing, Oh' |
| | [Three verses in D with Finale] |

This is all the information on this recording that is currently available. Until a copy of the complete recording turns up, it will remain a mystery.

11¾″ Pathe "Hill-and-Dale" record. From the complete recording of *The Yeomen of the Guard* with Amy Evans, 1907.

### H.M.S. PINAFORE
**Russell Hunting Record Company**
Excerpts on 11 'Sterling' Gold-Moulded Cylinders
1s.0d. each

| | |
|---|---|
| 940 | Overture. Imperial Infantry Band |
| 941 | Opening Chorus ("25 voices"!) |
| 942 | 'I'm Called Little Buttercup'. . . . . . . Ada Florence |
| 943 | 'A Maiden Fair to See' . . . . . . . . . . . Walter Hyde |
| 944 | 'I am the Captain of the Pinafore' . . . . . . . . Harry Dearth |
| 945 | 'When I was a Lad' . . . . . . . . . . . . . M. Anderson |
| 946 | Finale, Act I |
| 947 | Selection London Orchestral Band |
| 948 | 'Never Mind the Why and Wherefore' . . . . . . . . Ada Florence, Ernest Pike, Water Hyde |
| * | |
| 950 | 'He is an Englishman' . . . . . . . . . . . Harry Dearth, Bernard Turner |
| 951 | 'Farewell, My Own' |

*Number 949 is omitted from the sequence

### H.M.S. PINAFORE
**Odeon Company, 1908**
Complete on ten 10¾" double-sided records
in album with booklet, £2.10s.0d.
single records, 5s.0d.

Side Numbers: 44872-82, 44937-8, 66034, 66063
Matrix Numbers: Lx 2153-4, 2160-66, 2171-3, 2177-9, 2192-4, 2197, 2220
Catalogue Numbers: 0437-0446

| | |
|---|---|
| Sir Joseph Porter | . . . . . . . . . . . . . . . Willie Rouse |
| Captain Corcoran | . . . . . . . . . . . . . Harry Dearth |
| Ralph Rackstraw. | . . . . . . . . . . . . . . Walter Hyde |
| Dick Deadeye | . . . . . . . . . . . . . . Harry Thornton |
| Boatswain | . . . . . . . . . . . . . . Alfred Cunningham |
| Bill Bobstay. | . . . . . . . . . . . . . . . W. Anderson |
| Josephine | . . . . . . . . . . . . . . . . . . Elsa Sinclair |
| Hebe. | . . . . . . . . . . . . . . . . . . . . Miss Burnett |
| Little Buttercup. | . . . . . . . . . . . . . . . Ada Florence |

Much of this recording is transposed down – often as much as a third – primarily for the benefit of Walter Hyde and Harry Dearth. It is nevertheless, a fine recording, and almost complete, lacking only the overture, the entr'acte, part of the First Act Finale and 'A British Tar'.

Willie Rouse does not sing in the Act II Finale (Lx2220) which was apparently re-recorded at the first recording session of The Mikado.

*THE MIKADO*
**Odeon Company, 1908**
Complete on twelve 10¾" records
in album with booklet, £3.0s.0d.
single records, 5s.0d.

Side Numbers: 66035-56, 66057-9
Matrix Numbers: Lx 2221-3, 2225-7, 2237-49, 2261, 2276
Catalogue Numbers: 0425-0436

The Mikado. . . . . . . . . . . . . . . . . . . Harry Dearth
Nanki-Poo . . . . . . . . . . . . . . . . . . . . . Walter Hyde
Ko-Ko . . . . . . . . . . . . . . . . . . . . . Walter Passmore
Pooh-Bah. . . . . . . . Harry Thornton, Harry Dearth
Pish-Tush. . . . . . . . Harry Dearth, Harry Thornton
Yum-Yum . . . . . . . . . . . . . . . . . . . . . Elsa Sinclair
Pitti-Sing . . . . . . . . . . . . . . . . . . . . . Ada Florence
Peep-Bo . . . . . . . . . . . . . . . . . . . . . Maude Perry
Katisha. . . . . . . . . . . . . . . . . . . ; . . . . . Ada Florence

Aside from occasional doubling up in a few of the ensembles, the casting is generally consistent. The recording is complete, omitting only the overture, two sections of the First Act Finale, and (inexplicably) 'The Moon and I'. 'Here's a How-de-do' is encored. This recording was issued on both yellow and wine coloured labels. Different takes were sometimes used in the later issue.

10¾" Odeon. From the complete recording of *The Mikado* with Walter Passmore, 1908.

## THE GRAMOPHONE COMPANY
### Complete Recordings – 1917-1936

Henry Lytton as King Gama with J.M. Gordon, Gilbert's last stage manager, in 1920.
(Courtesy of the Ray Mander and Joe Mitchenson Theatre Collection)

In March of 1917 the Gramophone Company began to discuss the possibility of making a new series of Gilbert and Sullivan recordings. By July an agreement was signed with Rupert D'Oyly Carte for his "assistance" on a new recording of *The Mikado*. Under the terms of this agreement Rupert D'Oyly Carte would lend his music director and stage manager (then Walter Hann and J.M. Gordon) to the Gramophone Company to supervise the recording sessions. This would permit the Gramophone Company to advertise "recorded under the direction of Mr Rupert D'Oyly Carte", even though not a single performer from the D'Oyly Carte Company was going to appear on the recording. The Gramophone Company had decided to use singers exclusively from its stable of 'gramophone artists'. Even though the veteran Savoyards Henry Lytton, Leo Sheffield and Bertha Lewis were alive and well and performing *The Mikado* on tour, not one of them was chosen to appear in this first recording made "under the direction of Mr Rupert D'Oyly Carte"!

*The Mikado* was recorded in July and August of 1917, and issued in March 1918 with a cast that included Robert Radford, George Baker and Edna Thornton – fine artists to be sure, but artists who had never performed with the D'Oyly Carte Opera Company, and were not likely to.

Nevertheless, in March of 1919 a second agreement was signed by the Gramophone Company and Rupert D'Oyly Carte, under which four more operas would be recorded over the next three years. Under this agreement *The Gondoliers* was recorded in June 1919, again with *only* Gramophone Company artists in the cast.

To justify the use of its own singers, the Gramophone Company could quote reviews such as this:

> It goes without saying that in such superlative hands – or rather voices – a good deal of the music takes on a new meaning to most of us, and those who remember the original production at the Savoy in 1885 with the inimitable George Grossmith and Rutland Barrington as Koko and Pooh-Bah respectively, will probably experience a pleasant shock at hearing singers with real voices, for, great artists as were both the above-named gentlemen, no-one could claim for them much in the way of vocal beauty. Robert Radford's sonorous bass makes him a new creation of Pooh-Bah... and George Baker is another fine artist, and the way he does general utility man is a great tribute to his versatility.*
>
> – *Talking Machine News*, April 1918

The Gramophone Company had had a policy of using its own recording artists (as opposed to stage artists) which went back to the beginning of the century. If there was one field in which the Gramophone Company was *not* a pioneer, it was in original cast recordings.

After the First War Rupert D'Oyly Carte re-organized the Opera Company and in the autumn of 1919 was planning a return engagement in London, the Company's first appearance there in eleven years. The Company was scheduled to open at the Prince's Theatre on 29 September. As a result of the D'Oyly Carte Company's presence in London, pressure began to build on the Gramophone Company to use D'Oyly Carte singers in future recordings.

For while the Gramophone Company was holding to its policy of making records with only recording artists, the Columbia company was beginning to recognize "an increasing tendency for the public to demand records of theatrical musical productions by the artists whose names are associated with the theatres themselves." [*Talking Machine News*, September 1919] Columbia therefore lost no time in making arrangements with various leading West End managements to record their

*George Baker as 'general utility man' sang Ko-Ko, and part of the role of Pish-Tush. There was little attempt at continuity of casting in this first recording made under D'Oyly Carte 'supervision'.

current musical productions with members of the original casts. "What, for example, would not some of us give," a 1919 Columbia press release asked, "for a set of records by the original artists in such old favourites as the Savoy Opera, the plays when the sacred light of burlesque was first lighted at the old Gaiety, the 'Geisha' and the like."

In the middle of Columbia's original cast campaign, the D'Oyly Carte Opera Company opened with *The Gondoliers* at the Prince's Theatre, and the Gramophone Company released its recording of *The Gondoliers* with a non-D'Oyly Carte cast. The Gramophone Company's publicity department found itself reduced to the following gibberish to justify its use of its own singers:

> The records of the opera now issued by "His Master's Voice" are unique and of supreme historic interest, since they have been recorded under the direct supervision of Mr Rupert D'Oyly Carte, with the assistance of his company, and some of the finest English singers of the day. Thus the real tradition of the Gilbert and Sullivan days, as established by the author and composer, with Mr D'Oyly Carte of the original Savoy productions, has been perpetuated in these records, which thus have special authority, while as artistic productions they are equally remarkable.

It was upon the release of this recording with "some of the finest English singers of the day" that the Columbia Company made an offer to re-record *The Mikado* with an all D'Oyly Carte cast – what a recording that would have made – in 1919! Unfortunately, Rupert D'Oyly Carte's 1917 agreement with the Gramophone Company forbade the re-recording of *The Mikado* for ten years.

Columbia then approached some of the D'Oyly Carte artists themselves in the hope of finding some way around the new agreement with the Gramophone Company which only covered four operas. The Gramophone Company was not amused. They had been planning to record *The Yeomen of the Guard* in the beginning of 1920, again using only their own artists. However, because of the threat from Columbia, they agreed to make test recordings of four D'Oyly Carte singers, Henry Lytton, Leo Sheffield, Bertha Lewis and Derek Oldham; and in early November 1919, these artists recorded the following songs from *The Gondoliers* (the opera just recorded) and *The Yeomen of the Guard* (the opera to be recorded):

| | | |
|---|---|---|
| 'There Lived a King' . . . . . . . . . . . . . . . . . | Leo Sheffield | Ho5407ae |
| 'Is Life a Boon?' . . . . . . . . . . . . . . . . . . . | Derek Oldham | Ho5408ae |
| 'In Enterprise of Martial Kind' | | Ho5409ae |
| . . . . . . . Henry Lytton | | |
| 'I've Jibe and Joke' | | Ho5410ae |
| 'When our Gallant Norman Foes' . . . . . . . . . . . . . . . . . | | |
| | Bertha Lewis (12″) | Ho4124af |

All of these records were made with orchestra conducted by G.W. Byng, Music Director of the Gramophone Company. None was ever issued.

Leonard Petts, in his paper, *A Backstage Look at the Acoustic Gilbert and Sullivan Opera Recordings*, states that "On November 28 1919, these test records were played over to the British Sales Committee. The Minutes of this meeting dourly note:

> The Committee did not think that any of these, with the exception of Derek Oldham, would be of any use in forming the cast of the Gilbert and Sullivan operas.

"The entire matter was carefully considered and discussed. The Committee making the incredible pronouncement that the results obtained from the tests of the D'Oyly Carte artists, the Company would be lowering the standards of the next opera recording if members of the D'Oyly Carte were used."

The Gramophone Company had spoken. Thus *The Yeomen of the Guard, The Pirates of Penzance, Patience,* and *Iolanthe* were made with primarily Gramophone Company casts. The D'Oyly Carte management refused to permit its artists to record for another company with the unfortunate result that posterity lost the opportunity of hearing Henry Lytton, Leo Sheffield and Bertha Lewis in several of their greatest roles.

In 1922, however, Rupert D'Oyly Carte's new music director, Harry Norris, replaced George Byng as conductor of *H.M.S. Pinafore*, the next opera to be recorded. Three D'Oyly Carte artists, Bertha Lewis, Sydney Granville and Darrell Fancourt joined the cast.

In 1924 the D'Oyly Carte Opera Company played another highly successful season (February to July) at the Prince's Theatre, London. During that time *Ruddigore* was recorded with a nearly complete cast of D'Oyly Carte artists – minus unfortunately Henry Lytton. He was still supplanted for recording purposes by George Baker. Lytton had been judged too old to record the youthful role of Robin Oakapple, although he still played him on the stage.

In 1925 *Princess Ida* was recorded, and for the first time a *complete* complement of D'Oyly Carte artists was employed, including Henry Lytton as the aged King Gama.

It was then intended to record *Trial by Jury* and *The Sorcerer*, and eventually *Cox and Box*. But by 1926 the new process of electric recording had been adopted in Britain, and the Gramophone Company and Rupert D'Oyly Carte decided to record the operas all over again, beginning with

*The Mikado.* A new agreement was drawn under which ten operas would be recorded using D'Oyly Carte principals wherever possible. In fact, the only D'Oyly Carte principal who was not regularly used was Henry Lytton who, because of his age (he was 70 in 1930) was permitted to record only four of his famous roles.

The D'Oyly Carte Company continued to record for the Gramophone Company until 1936. After 1923 the operas were superbly cast. All of these recordings were supervised by J.M. Gordon, the last stage manager to work with W.S. Gilbert. There is, consequently, a high degree of authenticity and virtuosity on these early complete recordings. Most of those made between 1924 and 1932 have never been bettered. The earlier sets, however, those made by artists of the Gramophone Company, whether they were recorded "under the direction of Mr Rupert D'Oyly Carte" or not, are generally disappointing.

## THE GRAMOPHONE COMPANY RECORDINGS (1917-1936)

### Acoustic Sets

1917
*The Mikado*
HMV D 2-12, Victor Blue Label 55181-91*
Arthur Wood, cond., with George Baker, Robert Radford, John Harrison, Violet Essex, Edna Thornton.

1919
*The Gondoliers*
HMV D 36-46
Arthur Wood, cond., with George Baker, Robert Radford, John Harrison, Violet Essex, Bessie Jones, Edna Thornton.

1920
*The Yeomen of the Guard*
HMV Album Series 12,** D481-485, 496-501
G.W. Byng, cond., with George Baker, Robert Radford, Peter Dawson, Derek Oldham, Violet Essex, Nellie Walker, Edna Thornton.

1920
*The Pirates of Penzance*
HMV Album Series 9, D 504-514
G.W. Byng, cond., with George Baker, Peter Dawson, Ernest Pike, Violet Essex, Edna Thornton.

1921
*Patience*
HMV Album Series 8, D 563-571
G.W. Byng, cond., with George Baker, Frederick Ranalow, Peter Dawson, Ernest Pike, Violet Essex, Edna Thornton.

*Of the acoustic sets, only *The Mikado* and *H.M.S. Pinafore* were issued by Victor in America.
**HMV Album series numbers were assigned from 1929 on, after the first two albums above had been withdrawn.

1922                            *Iolanthe*
                    HMV Album Series 6, D 632-641
G.W. Byng, cond., with George Baker, Robert Radford, Sydney Granville, Peter
Dawson, Derek Oldham, Violet Essex, Nellie Walker, Edna Thornton.

1922                          *H.M.S. Pinafore*
          HMV Album Series 5, D 724-731; Victor Blue Label 55232-39
Harry Norris, cond., with Frederick Ranalow, Sydney Granville, Darrell Fancourt,
Frederick Hobbs, Walter Glynne, Bessie Jones, Bertha Lewis.

The complete casts of these recordings are given in Rollins and Witts, (see bibliography) pps. X-XIII.

1924                            *Ruddigore*
                    HMV Album Series 11, D 878-886
Harry Norris, cond., with George Baker, Leo Sheffield, Darrell Fancourt, Derek
Oldham, Elsie Griffin, Eileen Sharp, Bertha Lewis.

1925                          *Princess Ida*
                    HMV Album Series 10, D 977-986
Harry Norris, cond., with Henry Lytton, Leo Sheffield, Sydney Granville, Darrell
Fancourt, Derek Oldham, Winifred Lawson, Eileen Sharp, Bertha Lewis.

**Electric Sets**

1926                          *The Mikado*
          HMV Album Series 38, D 1172-82; Victor Album C 12, 35860-70*
Harry Norris, cond., with Henry Lytton, Leo Sheffield, George Baker, Darrell
Fancourt, Derek Oldham, Elsie Griffin, Doris Hemingway, Bertha Lewis.

1927                          *The Gondoliers*
          HMV Album Series 48, D 1134-45; Victor Album C 16, 11188-99
Harry Norris, cond., with Henry Lytton, Leo Sheffield, George Baker, Derek
Oldham, Aileen Davies, Winifred Lawson, Bertha Lewis.

1928                          *Trial by Jury*
          HMV Album Series 71, D 1469-72; Victor Album C 4, 9314-17
Harry Norris, cond., with Leo Sheffield, George Baker, Derek Oldham, Winifred
Lawson.

1929                      *The Yeomen of the Guard***
          HMV Album Series 74, D 1549-59; Victor Album C 17, 11220-30
Malcom Sargent, cond., with George Baker, Leo Sheffield, Peter Dawson, Derek
Oldham, Winifred Lawson, Nellie Briercliffe, Dorothy Gill.

1929                      *The Pirates of Penzance***
          HMV Album Series 83, D 1678-88; Victor Album C 6, 9607-17
Malcolm Sargent, cond., with George Baker, Leo Sheffield, Peter Dawson, Derek
Oldham, Elsie Griffin, Dorothy Gill.

*This early electric recording was issued on the Victor Black Label before the Victor Album Series was commenced.
The Black Label numbers were retained, and the album was pressed in America on inferior (noisy) Black Label
material until it was withdrawn after 1936. [The other electric sets were issued by Victor on superior material on the
wine coloured 'Orthophonic' label.]
**The D'Oyly Carte Company was on tour in American when these recordings were made. Hence the presence of a
large number of non-D'Oyly Carte members in the casts. Leo Sheffield, having recently retired from the Company,
was apparently still available for recording purposes.

1930                                      *Iolanthe*
                  HMV Album Series 89, D 1785-95; Victor Album C 10, 9708-18
          Malcolm Sargent, cond., with George Baker, Sydney Granville, Leslie Rands,
          Darrell Fancourt, Derek Oldham, Winifred Lawson, Nellie Briercliffe, Bertha
          Lewis.

1930                                   *H.M.S. Pinafore*
                  HMV Album Series 100, D 1844-52; Victor Album C 13, 9937-45
          Malcolm Sargent, cond., with Henry Lytton, George Baker, Sydney Granville,
          Darrell Fancourt, Charles Goulding, Elsie Griffin, Bertha Lewis.

1930                                      *Patience*
                  HMV Album Series 106, D 1909-18; Victor Album C 14, 11070-79
          Malcolm Sargent, cond., with George Baker, Leslie Rands, Darrell Fancourt,
          Derek Oldham, Winifred Lawson, Bertha Lewis.
          [Bertha Lewis died in a motor accident in May 1931.]

1931                                      *Ruddigore*
                  HMV Album Series 143, DB 4005-13; Victor Album C 19, 11510-18
          Malcolm Sargent, cond., with George Baker, Sydney Granville, Darrell Fancourt,
          Derek Oldham, Muriel Dickson, Nellie Briercliffe, Dorothy Gill.

1932                                    *Princess Ida*
                  HMV Album Series 169, DB 4016-25; Victor Album C 20, 11596-605
          Malcolm Sargent, cond., with Henry Lytton, Richard Watson, George Baker,
          Darrell Fancourt, Derek Oldham, Muriel Dickson, Nellie Briercliffe, Dorothy
          Gill.

1936                                    *The Mikado*
                  HMV Album Series 260, DB 4038-48; Victor Album C 26, 11961-71
          Isidore Godfrey, cond., with Martyn Green, Sydney Granville, Leslie Rands,
          Darrell Fancourt, Derek Oldham, Brenda Bennett, Marjorie Eyre, Josephine
          Curtis.

                               **Abridged Sets (10″)**

1931                              *The Yeomen of the Guard*
                            HMV Album Series 125, B 3799-3804
          Malcolm Sargent, cond., with George Baker, Sydney Granville, Derek Oldham,
          Muriel Dickson, Beatrice Elburn, Nellie Walker.

1931                             *The Pirates of Penzance*
                            HMV Album Series 126, B 3846-51
          Malcolm Sargent, cond., with George Baker, Sydney Granville, Darrell Fancourt,
          Derek Oldham, Muriel Dickson, Bertha Lewis.*

1931                                 *The Gondoliers*
                            HMV Album Series 127, B 3866-71
          Malcolm Sargent, cond., with George Baker, Sydney Granville, Leslie Rands,
          Derek Oldham, Muriel Dickson, Beatrice Elburn, Nellie Walker.

*In this recording Bertha Lewis sings only the trio from Act II, and a few lines in the Act I and II Finales.

1933                                    *The Sorcerer*\*\*
HMV Album Series 193, B 8054-59; Victor Album C 21, 4258-63
Isidore Godfrey, cond., with George Baker, Leslie Rands, Darrell Fancourt, Derek
Oldham, Muriel Dickson, Dorothy Gill.

\*\*The four abridged sets were issued in England in the Plum Label which was pressed on inferior material. Only *The Sorcerer* was issued in America where it was pressed on superior material with quieter surfaces.

# THE MIKADO ON FILM

In 1938 *The Mikado* became the first Gilbert and Sullivan opera to be
filmed (première, Leicester Square Theatre, London, 12 January 1939). It
was produced by Geoffrey Toye, who had conducted the D'Oyly Carte
Company for a few seasons in the twenties, and who wrote the new
overture to *Ruddigore*. Curiously enough the film still surfaces in cinema
circles where it is of interest as one of the earliest colour films ever
made!

The cast includes Martyn Green (Ko-Ko), Sydney Granville (Pooh-
Bah), Gregory Stroud (Pish-Tush) and Elizabeth Nickell-Lean (Pitti-
Sing), all current or former members of the D'Oyly Carte Company.
Geoffrey Toye conducted the D'Oyly Carte Chorus and the London
Symphony Orchestra.

*The Mikado* was filmed during J. M. Gordon's last season with the
Company, and preserves a visual record of some traditional stage business
which has since disappeared. The film is unique for the performance of
Sydney Granville, the only Savoyard to work with Gilbert and appear in a
Gilbert and Sullivan film. What is more the film preserves the only known
example of Gilbert's dialogue spoken by someone who worked with
him.

When the copyright on the film expires in 1990, the entire legacy of the
Savoyards will belong to the public.

# REISSUES by PEARL RECORDS

## The Art of the Savoyard [vol. I]
### 3-LPs GEM 118-120

RICHARD TEMPLE
'The Mikado's Song'
'I am a Pirate King'
'I am a Friar of Orders Grey'

SCOTT RUSSELL
'Would You Know the Kind of Maid'
'A Tenor Can't do Himself Justice'

ILKA von PALMAY
'Butterfly'

ISABEL JAY
'Poor Wand'ring One'

JOHN COATES
'Take a Pair of Sparkling Eyes'

HENRY LYTTON
'The Laughing Songe' (1900)
'The Curate's Song'
'None Shall Part Us'
'The Yeomen of England'
'Imagination'
'If You Give Me Your Attention'
'Whene'er I Poke Sarcastic Joke'

COURTICE POUNDS
'When a Pullet is Plump'

RUTH VINCENT
'Waltz Song'

ROBERT EVETT
'Is Life a Boon?'
'Free from his Fetters Grim'
'The English Rose'
'A Sprig of Rosemary'

WALTER PASSMORE
'The Fish Song'
'The Big Brass Band'
'Imagination'
'Bunthorne's Song' (1900)
'I've Got a Little List'
'I Have a Song to Sing Oh'
'A Private Buffoon'

CHARLES WORKMAN
'The Major-General's Song'
'Softly Sighing to the River'
'The Nightmare Song'
'If You Give Me Your Attention'
'Tit Willow'
'First You're Born'
'The Small Street-Arab'

LEO SHEFFIELD
'Oh Why Am I Moody and Sad?'
'I Once was a Very Abandoned Person'

BERTHA LEWIS
'There Grew a Little Flower'
'Come Mighty Must'

SYDNEY GRANVILLE
'He is an Englishman'

Interview with GEORGE BAKER
The famous baritone reminisces about the Savoyards he has known and worked with.

## The Art of the Savoyard, [vol. II]
### 2-LPs GEM 280-281

ARTHUR SULLIVAN
 Message to Thomas Edison

RUTLAND BARRINGTON
 'The Moody Mariner'

RICHARD TEMPLE
 'Non Piu Andrai' (in English)

SAVOY OPERA CHORUS
 'A Heavy Dragoon'
 *Patience*, Finale

AMY AUGARDE
 'I'm Called Little Buttercup'

HENRY LYTTON
 'The Curate's Song'
 'Four Jolly Sailormen'

J.G. ROBERTSON
 'Sigh No More, Ladies'

ESTHER PALLISER
 'The Sweetest Flower that blows'

WALTER PASSMORE
 'Bunthorne's Song' (1900)
 'My Name is John Wellington Wells'
  (1900)
 'The Judge's Song'
 'The Nighmare Song'
 'A Policeman's Lot'
 'If I Were Vanderbilt'

SCOTT RUSSELL
 'The Drinking Song'
 'Take a Pair of Sparkling Eyes'

ILKA von PALMAY
 'Madrigal'
 'A Little Bit of String'

CHARLES WORKMAN
 'Softly Sighing to the River'

FLORENCE ST. JOHN
 'He Loves Me, He Loves Me Not'

ELLEN BEACH YAW
 'The Laughing Song'
 Cadenza from *Etoile du Nord*

RICHARD GREEN
 'Two Little Irish Songs'

HAROLD WILDE
 'A Wand'ring Minstrel I'
 'Is Life a Boon?'

AMY EVANS
 'I Have a Song to Sing Oh'
 'A Man Who Would Woo a Fair Maid'
  (Trio)

CLAUDE FLEMING
 'The Call of the Sea'

LEO SHEFFIELD
 'Some Years Ago' (*Princess Ida*)

JULIUS LIEBAN
 'Bachstelzchenlied' (Tit Willow)

LILLIAN RUSSELL
 'Come Down Ma Evening Star'

## C.H. Workman's Gilbert and Sullivan
### GEM 135

'The Judge's Song'
'My Name is John Wellington Wells'
'When I was a Lad'
'The Major-General's Song'
'Softly Sighing to the River'
'Bunthorne's Song'
'The Law is the True  Embodiment'
'When I Went to the Bar'
'The Nightmare Song'
'If You Give Me Your Attention'

'When'er I Poke Sarcastic Joke'
'Tit Willow'
'I Have a Song to Sing Oh'
'I've Jibe and Joke'
'A Private Buffoon'
'In Enterprise of Martial Kind'
'I Stole the Prince'
'First You're Born'
'Some Seven Men Form An Association'
'The Small Street-Arab'

## The Art of Henry Lytton
### GEM 197

'The Laughing Song' (1905)
'He Was a Sailor'
'The Dotlet of My Eye'
'Two Little Chicks'
'Me and Mrs. Brown'
'Quarrelling'
'Peace, Peace'
'Everybody's Awfully Good to Me'
'When I Marry Amelia'
'Archie, Archie'
'By the Shore of the Mediterranean'
'My Cosy Corner Girl'
'Make it Up'
'You'd Better Ask Me'

'Four Jolly Sailormen'
'Imagination'
'The Yeomen of England'
'The Curate's Song'
'None Shall Part Us'
'If You Give Me Your Attention'
'Whene'er I Poke Sarcastic Joke'
'I've Got a Little List'
'Tit Willow'
'In Enterprise of Martial Kind'
'When I Was a Lad'

*The Mikado*
## The Complete 1908 Odeon Recording
### GEM 198

With Walter Passmore, Harry Dearth, Walter Hyde, Elsa Sinclair, Ada Florence.

## Sullivan without Gilbert
### GEM 279

This Album includes all seven selections from the 1908-13 recording of *The Golden Legend* sung by Percival Allen, Alice Lakin, Edna Thornton, John Harrison, Robert Radford. Other songs on the album include:

ANDREW BLACK
'King Henry's Song' (*Henry VIII*)

IAN COLQUHOUN
'The Absent-Minded Beggar'

WILLIAM GREEN
'The Sailor's Grave'

DAVID BISPHAM
'Ho Jolly Jenkin' (*Ivanhoe*)
'Woo Thou Thy Snowflake' (*Ivanhoe*)

EDITH EVANS
'Lord of Our Chosen Race' (*Ivanhoe*)

HERBERT TEALE
'Come Gentle Sleep' (*Ivanhoe*)

EDNA THORNTON
'Love Not the World' (*The Prodigal Son*)

EVAN WILLIAMS
'How Many Hired Servants'
(*The Prodigal Son*)

HARRY DEARTH
'The Drinking Song' (*The Rose of Persia*)

ROBERT RADFORD
'I Would I Were a King'

PERCIVAL ALLEN, etc. [Quartet]
Madrigal from *Haddon Hall*

# BIBLIOGRAPHY

Applebaum, Stanley, *Show Songs from 'The Black Crook' to 'The Red Mill'*. Dover Publications, New York, 1974

Bauer, Robert, *Historical Records*. Sidgwick and Jackson, London, 1947

Barnett, John R., *Voices of the Past*, Vol. I. The Oakwood Press, Lingfield, Surrey, 1955

Bispham, David, *A Quaker Singer's Recollections*. New York, 1920

Brown, James D., and Stratton, Stephen, S., *British Musical Biography*. Chadfield and Son, Derby, 1897

Diaries of Sir Arthur Sullivan [1880-1900]. MS, Yale University

Gaisberg, F.W., *Music on Record*. Robert Hale Ltd., London, 1946

Girard, Victor and Barnes, Harold M., *Vertical-Cut Cylinders and Discs*. British Institute of Recorded Sound, London, 1971

Grain, Corney, *Corney Grain by Himself*. John Murray, London, 1888

*The Green Room Book*. 1907, T. Sealey Clark, London

Grossmith, George [Jr.], *G. G.*, Hutchinson, London, 1933

Kutch, K.J., and Riemans, Leo, *A Concise Biographical Dictionary of Singers*. Chilton Book Co., New York, 1969

Moore, Jerrold Northrop, *A Voice in Time*. Hamish Hamilton, London, 1976

Moses, Julian Morton, *Collectors' Guide to American Recordings, 1895-1925*. American Record Collectors' Exchange, New York, 1949

Petts, Leonard, *A Back Stage Look at the Acoustic Gilbert and Sullivan Recordings*. [a paper delivered at Syracuse University, November 1983] MS, 1983

Ponder, Winifred, *Clara Butt, her Life-Story*. George C Harrap, London, 1928

Rollins, Cyril and Witts, R. John, *The D'Oyly Carte Opera Company in Gilbert and Sullivan Operas*. Michael Joseph, London, 1962

Rust, Brian, *London Musical Shows on Record, 1897-1978*. General Gramophone Publications, London, 1977

Scott, Clement, *From the Bells to King Arthur*. J. Maqueen, London, 1896

Scott, Michael, *The Record of Singing to 1914*. Duckworth, London, 1977

Stedman, Jane, *Gilbert Before Sullivan*. University of Chicago Press, Chicago, 1967

Terriss, Ellaline, *Just a Little Bit of String*, Hutchinson, London, 1955

Wearing, J.P., *The London Stage, 1890-1900*. The Scarecrow Press, Metuchen, New Jersey, 1976

Wearing, J.P. *The London Stage, 1900-1910*. The Scarecrow Press, Metuchen, New Jersey, 1981

Webb, Graham, *The Disc Musical Box Handbook*. Faber and Faber, London, 1971

*Who Was Who in the Theatre*. 1912-1976. Gale Research Co., Detroit, 1978

Wyndham, H. Saxe, *Who's Who in Music*. I. Pitman and Sons, London, 1915

NOTES

NOTES